CW00741419

DHARAVI

This book is a collaborative project between the department of Art & Architecure at
the The Royal University College of Fine Arts in Stockholm, Sweden and the authors
with kind assistance from The Society for the Promotion of Area Resource Centres
(SPARC) in Mumbai, India. The book is produced by the Royal University College
of Fine Arts in Stockholm, Sweden.

Editing: Jonatan Habib Engqvist and Maria Lantz
Book design: Johan Rutherhagen
Translations: Jonatan Habib Engqvist
Proofreading: Mark McLaren

Published in 2009 by Academic Foundation
4772 / 23 Bharat Ram Road, (23 Ansari Road)
Darya Ganj, New Delhi – 110 002
India

Tel: +91-11-23245001, 02, 03, 04.
Fax: +91-11-23245005.
website: www.academicfoundation.com

Printed by JAK Printers Pvt. Ltd., Mumbai, India, 2009
Printed on Arctic Volume HighWhite 130 g, environmentally friendly paper from
Arctic Paper, Sweden.

ISBN 978-81-7188-792-7

THE ROYAL UNIVERSITY COLLEGE OF FINE ARTS
ART & ARCHITECTURE

DHARAVI

DOCUMENTING INFORMALITIES

ACADEMIC FOUNDATION

SPONSORS AND PARTNERS

First and foremost, *Dharavi: Documenting Informalities* is the result of passionate work by the authors. The architects and artists who have contributed to this book in close collaboration with the people of Dharavi have done so without claiming payment for their work.

However, this book would never have been possible without the financial support of the Royal University College's Artistic Development Funds for Artistic Research (κυ-medel) and a generous grant from the Division for Urban Development at the Swedish International Development Cooperation Agency (sIDA).

Contents

"Dreams are the stuff cities are made of"

ARCHITECT CHARLES CORREA

PREFACE

When work on this book started in 2006, we wanted it to become a chronicle of Dharavi. It was an attempt to tell the story of a specific informal settlement: a dwelling, where people and buildings have been shaped by the necessities of a specific environment in a particular site. Houses and workplaces have developed over generations. The memories of struggles, stories and dreams all intertwine these places.

Markets, alleys and the landscape itself were created as a result of actions and hard work, through negotiations and mutual needs. The purpose of this chronicle was to twist the informal society toward a formal one; to show the power in people's abilities, and to encourage politicians and stakeholders to listen to the inhabitants of Dharavi and encourage them to develop the neighbourhood further and provide what was lacking in infrastructure and services.

We could not have imagined that this book would be completed in the midst of a storm. The Master Plan – the idea to sell off the entire area – started to roll as we were editing this Dharavi chronicle. Politicians finally noticed Dharavi, but what they saw was a problem: the people living there. They also saw possibilities to get rich from the land. Dharavi and its 700,000 or so inhabitants were suddenly tossed around in big international business schemes conducted by powers far away from the dwellings of Dharavi.

Soon after our book was released, the film Slumdog Millionaire opened in cinemas all over the world. Parts of the film were shot in Dharavi. National Geographic made an exotic journey to the spot and The New York Times quoted our book. Dharavi became world famous. Dharavi is unique in many ways, but is no exception in the wider issues of housing shortages.

All over India and all over the globe there are communities similar to Dharavi. As urbanization keeps on accelerating, informal economies are also booming. The architecture of slums, favelas and shanty towns might, in one sense, be labelled as the dominant housing solution of contemporary urban life and are often located at the very centre of global economic systems. This is not a new development. All over Europe there are historical examples. The Old Town in Stockholm – once a rubbish dump, later became a concentration of shacks for the poor, and now serves as the foundations to some of the most expensive real estate in Sweden. Informal settlements can and will develop – if there is a political will.

Since the book was produced, we have returned to Dharavi on several occasions. A symposium was also organized in Stockholm entitled Informal Cities where architects and artists as well as grass-root activists discussed urbanization and informal settlements. People attended from South Africa, Brazil, The Philippines, India and Malawi. We heard common problems and listened to stories told in the presence of international politicians and decision-makers. We are currently planning an exhibition on this topic in Mumbai.

Our investigations into how art and architecture can contribute to social and political discussions are not merely academic projects. We have very concrete goals: to increase knowledge about informal living in cities; to suggest more participatory and inclusive descriptions of the urban poor; and to increase infrastructure in informal areas by searching out new collaborations and networks. In short – to sustain ability. By giving voice to the informal, this second, Indian edition of Dharavi: Documenting Informalities continues the discussion on how we can live, how we can dwell, together on this globe.

BY MARIA LANTZ AND JONATAN HABIB ENGQVIST
STOCKHOLM, IN AUGUST 2009

INTRODUCTION:

Mapping

This book is not a scientific study, nor is it fiction. To a large extent it contains images of urban poverty, of slums and of colourful people. Yet it does not claim to be either coffee-table fashion, or hard-hitting journalism. In fact to say what the book is not, is much easier than to affirm what it is. *Dharavi: Docmenting Informalities* is the result of a journey that began without agendas or intentions, and without any end result in mind. As such, our wish is to reflect the confusion and unanswered questions that we brought back from that journey, as well as to present our findings.

This is not to take away from the book its serious concerns. By using creative rather than scientific methods, by asking fundamental, sometimes naïve questions and by using personal storytelling and self-criticism, we have focused in on what the media has come to term "the biggest slum in Asia". While journalists usually stop there, we wanted to continue, to move on beyond the obvious.

BACKGROUND

During the spring of 2005 a group consisting of several artists, architects and writers travelled to India as part of the on-going Art & Architecture project based at the Royal University College of Fine Art in Stockholm. This program aimed to follow an artistic tradition of social engagement that can be traced back to Goya's etchings of the Napoleon war or Jacob Riis's photographs of New York during the late 1800s. After Riis published *How the Other Half Live* things changed. Living conditions for workers in Manhattan were brought to public attention, child labour came to an end, housing programs were developed and local government built more schools.

We decided to study the informal architecture and economy of Dharavi, Mumbai's city within a city, in a similar manner. The conditions in Dharavi are not just the concern of the local government of Maharastra. We are all connected to Dharavi, and Dharavi is connected to every corner of the world through merchandise and labour. Dharavi is like a seeding plant that can spread and flourish even where the ground has been bulldozed and covered with concrete.

Everyone on the planet is connected to one another. Not only through the abstract concepts of global warming and pollution, but also through simple things like a skirt, a button,

0:2

0:3

or a bag. In our homes, here in Stockholm, there are many things which have been produced in Dharavi. We take these items for granted: the leather patch at the back of a pair of jeans, the wheels that keep a suitcase rolling, the box we throw away once we've opened a gift. Through merchandise and global economic structures we are connected in a relationship that should be described as symbiotic, not anonymous. What goes on in Dharavi is therefore, morally and fundamentally, our concern. We are part of Dharavi and Dharavi is part of us.

Our impressions from this journey were strong – we touched and tasted and heard and smelt things that we could never have read about. But when we gathered to sum up our knowledge we realised how little we actually knew, there was an urge to move on and explore further. We started to collect material and kept in touch with some of the organizations that we met on our first trip in February and March 2005. After some time we decided to go back to Dharavi and during the next couple of months we prepared a new journey in the Spring of 2006. Two of the group went back for a third visit in 2007. We decided to focus on a case study of Dharavi. Our task was to document informalities.

WHY DOCUMENTATION?

From the dawn of colonialism, mapping has been of uttermost importance. Documents and maps serve those in power. Receipts, identity cards, social security registration certificates, addresses, passports and certified land ownership – all these institutionalized documents confirm one's existence in the eyes of the rulers and guarantee acceptance as a member of the formal society. One can, for instance, legally sell and buy a house, write a contract for subletting and renting or go to the bank to borrow money. But most importantly: one has the right to stay where one belongs. In order to reach these fundamental rights, documents are needed.

0:2   Bandits' Roost, 1890,
      Jacob A. Riis,
      glass lantern slide.
      The Jacob A. Riis
      Collection,

0:3   Women and children,
      Dharavi 2006.
      Maria Lantz
      Colour photograph.

Documentation serves as a proof of the prevailing order. What we learnt from the informal citizens of Dharavi, from people who do not have the legal rights to stay in the space
where they were born, was to use the same kind of methods as the formal society. Count the
people in the neighbourhood. Put numbers on the houses. Create addresses for each and
every family. Form a group of inhabitants and choose a local leader. Save money together.
Pinpoint mutual goals. Negotiate. Be aware of the local history. To play by the rules of the
"formal" you must formalize the informal. All of this could be summarized as "mapping" By
mapping we mean more than just claiming government rights. We mean actually forming
identities and creating methods of agency that can be used outside the usual parameters.
Dharavi's complex informal structures are part of why the neighbourhood is so fragile.
When we began to understand this, we decided to add to documentation which had already
been done by the local community in order to present Dharavi to the rest of the world. To
politicians, to companies, to the people like us who wear jeans sewn in Dharavi and to those
who simply are unaware about these dazzling aspects of India's booming economy.

In this book we use all the tools we have to document. We have been inspired by artists
who have personally engaged themselves like Yoko Ono, engaged politically like Martha
Rossler and Joseph Beuys but also land-artists like Robert Smithson, and Walter de Maria.
More specifically, the documentation techniques that have been used in relation to the
"dematerialized" art object or "informal" art, such as happenings, installations and land-art
have influenced our groups' methods in a productive manner. We tell the story about the
people we have met, their territory, their works and their organizations. Though most of the
images in the book only contain Westerners out of frame photographing Indians, the use
of the personal texts is an attempt to place the "I" of the photographers back into the frame,
to make the viewers aware of the context of each image, to remove the cliché aesthetics of
beautiful, mute images of poverty.

We have photographed streets and alleys, both good and bad examples of dense living. We have mapped out and formalized informal structures on the street Puna Valla,
investigated the leather workshops, climbed the re-location construction sites, followed the
saving-schemes and interviewed some of the people behind the new "Master Plan" Now we
see how our questions mirrored our concerns: how little we knew, how stupid we had been!

The Master Plan is difficult to grasp, and even more difficult to evaluate, especially for
outsiders. It is packaged as a "sustainable and legal" solution for a "slum free" Dharavi. In
the proposal, the area is divided into five different sectors, each to be developed separately
through overseas investments. The calculations also consider rehousing 60,000 families
to high-rise buildings where each family will be allotted 21 square metres with sanitation.
Rehousing is financed through a system which enables private investors to build cheaply
and to lease certain parts of their developments at high market prices. We do not know
how many people actually live in Dharavi, but 60,000 families is a low count. Normally,
60% of the area's official inhabitants would need to agree to this kind of transformation,
but the argument from the city planner's point of view, is that this is an unnecessary step in
Dharavi's case since the project already has received support from the government.

During our journey, a lot of things have happened in Dharavi. Back in the spring 2006 no
one believed that the so called Master Plan for Dharavi would go through, but an email from
Sundar Burra, the advisor and coordinator of SPARC and the man who first introduced us to

```
From:     s-@gmail.com
Subject:  Re: fund-raising
Date:     wednesday 7 feb 2007 07.38.07 GMT+01:00
To:       m-@kkh.se
Copy:     s-@vsnl.com, s-@sparcindia.org, a-@kkh.nu
```

Dear Maria,

It is good you are looking for funding for your book and
I am sure it will come through.

The sad part is that the Govt. of Maharashtra is supporting a plan to break up Dharavi into 5 sectors and invite
international bidders to redevelop it without regard for
people's ideas and participation. All of us are now busy
trying to stop this plan and suggest an alternative.

If we lose, Dharavi as you saw it will become a memory
and most of the poor people will be thrown out of there.

Affectionately,
Sundar

Dharavi told us that the Master Plan had started rolling. The threat of a complete demolition of the 1.75 square kilometre area of Dharavi had not been taken very seriously, but today the prices of land have risen to a level where the government of Maharastra is considering selling off the entire area. But on the 30th May 2007, The Government of Maharastra put out advertisements in the global press asking for "Expressions of Interest" in the redevelopment of Dharavi. Right now the land and the people of Dharavi are waiting. Huge bids have been placed by international companies. Those who have the correct documentation will be "bought out" and placed in tiny flats in high-rises. But for the rest of the population, the ones who rent or do not yet have "formal" housing, the future is very uncertain. So is the future of the workshops, the schools, the mosques, the temples, the markets. How can these structures survive in high-rise buildings? Job opportunities will definitely be lost in a neighbourhood where air-conditioned bank offices, parking lots and supermarkets will replace the local business of Dharavi today. Dharavi's destiny is uncertain. The only thing that is certain is that the lives of hundreds of thousands of people are about to be affected in a radical way.

This book has many voices, some of them contradictory. The past three years has engaged us all in the future of Dharavi. But at this point we find ourselves asking some fundamental questions:
How can a country, a government, sell off the homes of their own population?
How is it possible to put land and structures, built up over generations, under international bidding?
When a government acts this way, does this spell the end of a politics which can ever be changed by non-politicians?
In what way are we part of these actions and can we do anything about it?

This book maps Dharavi in at least two ways: first of all it documents the informal city using formal architectural methodologies. This place has developed in an extraordinary way, and we have a lot to learn from the many innovations and structures that are almost unique to Dharavi.

Secondly it maps our interest in the issues of slums, the people who live there and their conditions. The people of the wealthy North are watching. We are eager to understand. With this book we want to show that innocent non-experts have a right to be curious, have a right to take part. We hope this book can shape the way we as wealthy consumers think about our complex and mutual relation to Dharavi. The bottom line is that we need to take more responsibility. In order to do this, we want to learn from the grass root organizations.

The task we have given ourselves with this book is impossible and we are by no means claiming to solve any of Dharavi's fundamental problems. But if this book can map out some of the complex structures that we saw on our short visits and communicate a few of the creative, truly sustainable structures of this area, we have at least started a process.

We still have a lot to learn from Dharavi and we wish to thank the inhabitants of Dharavi and the organizations The Society for the Promotion of Area Resource Centres (SPARC), Slum Dwellers International Federation (SDIF) and Mahila Milan for their endless patience. We also want to thank the Royal University College of Fine Art in Stockholm and the Swedish International Development Cooperation Agency (SIDA) for their generous support without which none of this would have been possible. This book is evidence, both of what the people of Dharavi have taught us, but also of what we still need to understand.

STOCKHOLM, SPRING 2008

The authors i alphabetical order, with abriviations:
Sophie Allgårdh (SA), Stina Ekman (SE), Love Enqvist (LE), Anna Erlandson (AE), Jake Ford (JF), Jonatan Habib Engqvist (JHE), Jonas Jernberg (JJ), Martin Karlsson (MK), Maria Lantz (ML), Monika Marklinger (MM), Johan Widén (JW)

0:4

0:4 Discussing the Indian
edition and upcoming
exhibition at the Kamla
Raheja Vidyanidhi Insti-
tute for Architecture,
KRVIA in Mumbai,
February 2009.

CHAPTER 1:

THE WORLD – DHARAVI

The "Glocal" City

2006 marked the year when more than half of the world's population were living in cities. It is predicted that this shift will have as much impact on civilisation as the time when humanity moved from groups of hunter-gatherers to societies based on horticulture.

There are many reasons for this shift, a combination of economic structures, technology and globalization. One reason for urbanisation is the promise of the city itself. Cities contain the possibility of individual success, of adventure, of education and development. The city is a hub for business and money – but also for contemporary culture and inventions. People move to cities because they have ambitions. Dreams are what cities are built of, as Indian architect Charles Correa puts it.

It is not only the people who move to cities that cause expansion, cities themselves are developing from within. Mumbai is a perfect example of this city boom. From today until 2030 the population is estimated to double: from 16 to around 30 million inhabitants. Mumbai will face a huge problem: where will the population live? Like Manhattan in New York, Mumbai has limited land. The peninsula is surrounded by sea and land is extremely expensive. Unlike Manhattan, there is no surrounding land to bridge to. Especially during monsoon season, storms and rain can cut off the peninsula from the mainland with the exception of a narrow passage to the north.

Mumbai's success is also its dilemma. The booming economy has, to a greater extent, developed because of the informal economy and the underclass of workers who serve the city. But when land is so over-priced, the informal housing areas are usually torn down, and the poor are evicted. These evictions are not merely from one site to another, but more often far outside of the city. Mumbai faces questions that all cities will face sooner or later. The question of the right for poor people to live in cities, who the city is for and how can we live

The Global City
— STRATEGIC SITE / NEW FRONTIER

by Saskia Sassen

Beginning in the 1980s we see the partial rebuilding of cities as platforms for a rapidly growing range of globalized activities and flows, from economic to cultural and political. Cities emerge above all as strategic territorial moments of an increasingly electronic and globally dispersed economy. This also explains why as globalization expanded in the 1990s and onwards, the number of global cities also increased.

We can think of the global city as containing a state-of-the-art economic and regulatory platform for handling the far-flung global operations of firms and markets.

But the global city is also a space for new types of politics.

FIGHTING FOR THE RIGHT TO URBAN SPACE

One source for politics comes out of the fact that this state-of-the-art platform has to be made – it is made physically, occupying more and more urban space, it is made by the state's regulatory interventions, it is shaped by architects and planners making the appropriate built environments, by wood and metal workers ensuring the luxury look in homes and consumption spaces. In brief, the new glamour zones we see in global cities across the world require an often violent insertion of a whole new kind of urban space in an often crowded and dense older urban space.

In this process, inevitably, growing numbers of modest, low-profit, firms and households will be displaced, no matter how much their products and services are needed by large sectors of the city's population. This displacement tends to happen rapidly, but it can take years, or stagnate and then kick back in. In New York City, for example, this displacement created tens of thousands of homeless people, and a new phenomenon, homeless families, mostly mothers and their children. As they became visible on the streets of the city, the city developed ways to re-house them – the infamous homeless hotels paid for by the city, that is to say taxpayer's money going to pay for the damages produced by a high-profit, high-income economic sector. Eventually NY City's government also removed the homeless to more marginal areas of the city. Such displacements transform urban space from the civic to political. Politics become wired into urban space itself. And urban space becomes an actor in this conflict. This kind of displacement leads to a distinctive type of politics, a fight for access to urban space. This is a global fight that also plays out in the domains linked to the environment, public transport, public parks, etc.

However, anti-gentrification struggles are one example of this perspective on global politics. These struggles are not global because there is a global institution involved – such as the International Monetary Fund and the World Trade Organization. On the contrary, they are very local. They are about this building and that slum. Their globality stems from the fact that they happen in city after city worldwide. This is a fight between powerful global actors and the most vulnerable, local and often non-organized people fighting in their neighbourhoods, for their livelihoods.

The possibility of this strategic urban encounter becomes important when you consider that global capitalism is elusive, partly electronic. It is not like the factories in the old days, when workers could directly confront the owner. Today, it's not even clear who the owner is. The vulnerable have very few opportunities to engage with global capital. The politics of the rights to the city are one way in which they can act.

WHEN ECONOMIC GROWTH MEANS MORE RICH AND MORE POOR

A key feature of the new urban economy is a sharp increase in both very high-income jobs and very low-income jobs, and the shrinking of the older, modest middle-class. Before the 1980s, economic growth tended to mean the growth of a solid middle class. But the rise of a global corporate economy brings with it a sharp growth in the demand for top level professionals and growing numbers of super-profit making firms. These professionals and firms have the means, and often, the government support, to displace a whole variety of middle-level firms and workers. The growing demand for state of the art everything – from luxury offices and homes to the ultimate pot of caviar – reduces the options for the modest middle class to live in these cities. If they can, they leave.

The loss of the older middle classes has another negative effect for the city, often overlooked. The more of a city's income goes to the middle class, the greater the share that will re-circulate and be spent in the city itself, which has a growth effect on the city. Middle classes tend to spend more of their income than the very rich, who have so much that they invest most of it – and who knows in what and where.

But the top-level firms and households need all kinds of low-wage workers and the goods and services of low-profit firms. On Wall Street, for example, cleaning jobs are outsourced to immigrants. Luxury restaurants, shops and hotels, the opera and the theatre, all need battalions of low-wage workers. There is a whole new informal economy that is part of the global economy. For instance, the new luxury shops and homes often require very specialized woodwork (mostly done informally) and use designers who in turn use informal wood and metal shops. Much of this cannot be done through mass-manufacturing.

DEREGULATION AT THE TOP
IN-FORMALIZATION AT THE BOTTOM

The new informal economy is part of advanced capitalism, even when it does not look like it. This explains the particularly strong growth and dynamism of informal economies in global cities. And it helps to explain a mostly overlooked development: the proliferation of an informal economy of creative professional work in these cities – artists, architects, designers, software developers. The new informal economy is also emerging in global cities of the South, but there it is often submerged under the vast older informal economy – it is less visible than in the North.

The new types of in-formalization of work are the low cost equivalent of formal deregulation in finance, telecommunications and most other economic sectors in the name of flexibility and innovation. The difference is that while formal deregulation is costly and requires often large public and private funds, in-formalization is low-cost and largely on the backs of the workers and their households.

In my research on the new informal economies in global cities of the North I found that there is a set of mediating processes at work. One is the increased earnings inequality and the associated restructuring of consumption in high income groups and in very low income groups, both of which are more likely to use informally produced goods and services than the standard middle class. A second is the increased inequality in the profit-making capacities of different types of firms in a city. Critical here is the inability among many of the providers of the goods and services demanded by high-income households and by high profit-making firms, to keep on operating in global cities because of the high costs. Leading sectors have sharply bid up the prices of commercial space, labour, auxiliary services, and other basic business costs. In-formalizing part or all of these operations has turned out to be one of the ways in which the more modest firms could continue to function in these cities and meet the real and often expanded demand for their goods and services.

It is then the combination of growing inequality in earnings and growing inequality in the profit-making capabilities of different sectors in the urban economy which has promoted the in-formalization of a growing array of economic activities in the global cities of the North. These are integral conditions in the current phase of advanced capitalism as it materializes in major cities dominated by the new advanced services typically geared to world markets and characterized by extremely high profit-making capabilities. In the global cities of the North it becomes important to emphasize that these are not conditions imported from less developed countries via immigration, as is so often argued.

Secondly, the new emerging creative informal economy is also caught up in these spatio-economic inequalities even as its contents and projects are radically different from those of the manufacturing and service oriented informal economies. A city such as Berlin is a dramatic example of the mix of dynamics at work here. A large concentration of artists, designers, new media activists and a large concentration of newly emptied and unclaimed spaces as East Berlin was reincorporated.

On a more abstract level, three features stand out about informality in today's major cities. One is that in-formalizing production and distribution activities is a mode of incorporation into the advanced urban economy. The far more common belief is that the informal

1:2

economies in global cities of the North is an anachronism imported via lowly educated immigrants. What the version of this incorrect argument might be in a city like Mumbai is not clear to me. Second, in-formalizing creative work (whether of architects, craft-workers, metal workers, and so on) is one of the most entrepreneurial aspects of the urban economy – today's equivalent of past forms of the much praised economic creativity that cities make possible. Third, in-formalization is the low-cost equivalent of what at the top of the system we have called deregulation (of finance, telecommunications, etc.)

In sum, the new advanced urban economy incorporates a far larger mix of types of firms, workers, and economic spaces in the city than is usually recognised. Parts of the immigrant communities in the cities of the global North and parts of the shanty towns and slum areas of the global South are also part of the new advanced urban economy. But experiencing them as such is far more difficult than is the corporate complex of luxury office towers.

Beyond these articulations of new informal economies with advanced capitalism there is a simpler way to present cities as irreducible to a few sectors. They become company towns or urban plantations. Cities are among the most complex collective productions we have produced. They cannot be fully controlled. They are fuzzy logic systems. The multiple sub-economies that a large city contains all can make claims on urban space.

WHEN POLITICS BECOME URBAN AND INFORMAL

Large complex cities, are a frontier zone where an enormous mix of people converge. Those who lack power, those who are disadvantaged, outsiders, discriminated minorities, can gain presence in such cities, presence vis à vis power and presence vis à vis each other.

This signals, for me, the possibility of a new type of politics centred on new types of political actors. It is not simply a matter of having or not having power. There are new hybrid bases from which to act.

The space of the city is a far more concrete space for politics than that of the nation. It becomes a place where non-formal political actors can be part of the political scene in a way that is much more difficult at the national level. Nationally politics needs to run through existing formal systems: whether the electoral political system or the judiciary. Non-formal political actors are rendered invisible in the space of national politics. Cities, in contrast, can accommodate a broad range of political activities – squatting, demonstrations against police brutality, fighting for the rights of immigrants and the homeless, the politics of culture and identity, gay and lesbian politics. Much of this becomes visible on the street. Urban politics are concrete, enacted by people rather than dependent on massive media technologies.

The large city of today, especially the global city, emerges as a strategic site for these new types of operations. It is a strategic site for global corporate capital. But is is also one of the sites where the formation of new claims by informal political actors materialize and assume concrete forms.

SASKIA SASSEN

Saskia Sassen (Columbia University) is the author of *The Global City* (2001) and *Territory, Authority, Rights* (2006)

"'Belonging' is a basic emotional need – its associations are of the simplest order. From 'belonging' – identity – comes the enriching sense of neighbourliness. The short narrow street of the slum succeeds where spacious redevelopment frequently fails."

PETER SMITHSON
CIAM'S 1953 CONGRÈS D'ARCHITECTURE MODERNE

1:3

1:4

Zooming In

1:4

1:4

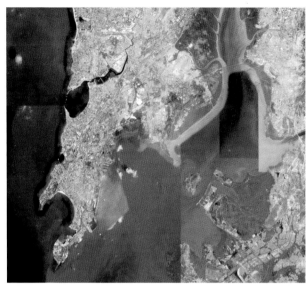

1:4   1:4

Mumbai is situated on the western coast of India in the state of Maharastra. Today foreigners usually arrive by airplane, but once this was the main entry port of ships from the West to India. Bom Bahia or Bon Bay – good harbour – the location for a safe port is obvious. The peninsula works as a pier and cuts off a bay from the rough Indian ocean.

When flying into the Mumbai airport the plane almost touches the rooftops of the nearby slum areas. One of them is Dharavi, the triangle-shaped city within the city, located just south of the Chatrapati Shivaji International airport and the marshlands of Mahim Creek. The aerial images from the Internet provided by NASA and Google Earth enable us to zoom in on the area from above.   *JHE*

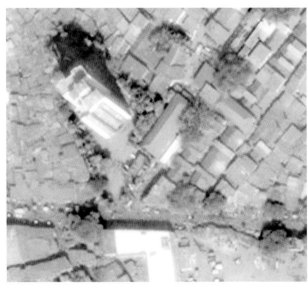

1:4   1:5

Who's afraid of the urban poor?

Fear should not be underestimated. When capitalism showers wealth onto the powerful, the fear of losing these things is always part of the bargain. The history of fear has yet to be written. Fear can give us an understanding of why we need security, social planning, commodities and to demonize others.

If fear was once concerned with what lay concealed in the darkness outside our homes, or how the anger of the gods would affect our crops, it now encompasses a completely different territory. The geography of fear is no longer limited to the space that surrounds us and hardly touches our relationship to God. Instead, new forms of distress have evolved.

When I read the newspaper or turn on my TV, I meet images of faraway places. Images projected into my living room and into my consciousness because they have a news value, because "something has happened". The images are almost always about war and conflict, about uprisings and

1:7

violence. These images represent a returning "truth" that the distant also is the dangerous. This "truth" that seems to characterise our time where knowledge has been replaced by media structures – facts by demonizing.

When I approached Dharavi from an air-conditioned car, something was activated from within my memory-bank. Through the images that I have been exposed to in the past, I recognised something. It seemed familiar, and I even thought that I knew something about it because of the images I had seen. This mistake was naturally fraught with consequences since knowledge is something other than recognition. Yet, as I passed by Dharavi the conclusion was instantaneous: this is slum. And slum means dirt and misery, something dangerous. It was something to fear. In this environment there were poor people that at any moment could throw themselves at me – a rich, white woman- could rob, assault, take revenge. I considered the probability that this was a place where the extremists of the future were

raised, where bombs were manufactured, where foul deeds were being schemed. Slum – means dread.

In her book *War and Photography*, Caroline Brothers deciphers the broader meaning of mass media images from faraway places. Her thesis is that images of war and misery or just of general poverty ultimately are about the construction of a common identity: "we". This "we" must infringe on and be a juxtaposition on "them", where the fear of this other is fundamental.

Today it seems that the idea of a common lifestyle has replaced the "we" within local communities. And one might claim that mass media fills a uniting function within a cultural sphere – regardless of national boundaries. Within this community, fear is ubiquitous. We know that we are living beyond our resources, on credit. It is, in Zygmut Bauman's words, a floating fear: a weak and undefined fear, it is everywhere and nowhere, a paralysing fear. From this condition, comfort can be found by trying to articulate, to

make the fear manageable. The most effective strategy for this is to place it outside, beyond our closest vicinities. This is why images from faraway places always look the same. The images help to create a canon or establish the distinction between "we" and "them".

What must be pointed out is difference itself. Similarities would dissolve boundaries and thereby destabilise our own position. In an anonymous, global world it seems as if the more fortunate constantly have to establish an advantage over the less fortunate in order to keep fear from seeping in. – "Take it easy, you're safe here. But over there – now that's dangerous!"

If one analyses where mass media images of the other come from, there will always be a focus on the cities. It is in cities that riots take place; the city is an arena for demonstrations and violence. We seldom see images from daily life. Instead, media is obsessed by the spectacular. Consequently one presupposes constant danger, perpetual war

and violence in these places. One outcome of this is the strengthening of prejudice and the demonizing of others.

In popular culture, this seeping fear is inspired by exotic and violent environments, almost an orientalism of the brutal, you might say. Terrorists and revolutionaries are chased through narrow alleys in slum-like environments, for example in computer games like Counter Strike. It is an image of the master's imagination, a fantasy that in reality describes only our imagined fear.

The frightened one attempts to create security, in games as well as in the physical environment. This can imply precise behavioural considerations: should I turn and run quickly or hunch and sneak forward? Travel in an armoured car or by taxi? Do I prepare for fight or flight? But above all, frightened people create security through building. "My home is my fortress"– the expression can be found all over Europe. The idea of home as a safe haven has characterized humans throughout history. The dominant class have always

created castles and forts, moats and walls. The labyrinth-like city could offer a greater security than the isolated palace, as long as people were living under fair conditions. In this density, the city, the Sovereign and the subjects could find a symbiosis, a relationship. This relationship was manifested in buildings. Such as in the old Medinian city, ancient Asian cities and in the medieval fortified cities of Europe.

The city can also be seen as an environment of negotiation. By developing an architectural and economic security from the outside world, individuals within this group also develop a sense of inclusion. In some ways similar to the sense that can be found within a clan: a "we" where loyalty and interdependency create solidarity. A form of union grows in such a place where trust is negotiated internally and is established in order to handle the fear of outside enemies. In a way, perhaps democracy was born here when, through sharing and distribution, individuals could create better possibilities for themselves.

The concept of the fortified city often strikes me when I visit contemporary city slum areas, whether they happen to be in Asia, Latin America or North Africa. The slum always has a boundary, toward a road, railway or some other barrier. To step over this line implies a step from an "outside", to an "inside". This certainly applies in Dharavi. For me it means entering a place where I do not belong. I am a stranger in this city inside a city. But if I am invited, I will soon be a guest and after the introduction rituals, I may also be accepted by those who reside in the area. A city slum area – a Fevela in Brazil, a Geccecoundo in Turkey, a slum-pocket in India or a shanty town in South Africa is a kind of fort. Here, as in the fortified city, the interdependency and security, is uniting and necessary. The flow of information is quicker than the wind: people live so close to each other that news travels along alleys, up stairs and into houses at the speed of lightning, faster than the fastest broadband. And I know that wherever I tread, everyone

1:7

knows who I am and who has invited me into their home. I know that I am being watched, judged and commented on. But I also feel secure in the knowledge that this system can protect me, for I too am encased in the codes of honour and respect of this community. Societies do not always abide by the national, general laws, but develop their own rules. For better or worse – for often local laws are created by the right of the powerful. But even the strong also need the respect of their neighbours in order to survive. So systems evolve

where rules are tested out in the same fashion as our common history has developed law over time. The worst form of punishment, sometimes worse than death, is excommunication. To be excluded from the common. In this constant wearing and tearing the city grows and transforms from inside, adapts, takes shape.

The informal city is in this respect less anonymous and better adapted than the formal city. There is elasticity and a local presence that the formalised city lacks. The fixed

systems and anonymity that we have learnt to live with and appreciate in the large modern cities are the result of a specialization where control and separation is the key.

When the modern city was established the city-plans where laid out. These plans allowed the city to be diversified and to grow. This was made possible through the abundance of cheap fuel. Oil was the key to the formation of cities. Dormitory suburbs where built in one place, offices in another and industries somewhere else. Modernity could solve the problems of waste, goods and services through transport and logistics. Communication between the various, specialised parts is one of the often forgotten distinguishing marks of the modern city.

With the development of private motoring there was a transformation in the landscape of the city, creating a typology of traffic flow. With the car, it was possible to transport oneself without resistance and contact with one's surroundings. The private automobile was a bubble, an extension of

the home, a transportable private sphere. But how did this affect fear? Through the car, people where cut off from their daily environment. Smells, tastes, textures and sounds no longer reached the driver and the fear of the world outside the vehicle's closed door grew stronger.

Today the buildings in a middle class area appear as if they hide military secrets. Surveillance-cameras, walls with sensors, dogs, electric fences, broken glass, barbed wire, double locks and security guards – all of these attributes

belong to a growing middle class all over the world. One of Sweden's most successful export companies produces fences and India is one of the most expansive markets. But what are they protecting themselves from, and why? Is it really necessary? Could it be different?

In many ways, what we find in the informal cities can be seen as a mirror image of all cities' historical development. But there is also a lot to be found here that points toward the future. In the informal city, for example in Dharavi, traffic

1.7

is extremely limited. There are a few larger roads that surround the area and some wider streets that cut through it, but generally speaking, the transportation within the area is conducted by bicycle, carts and sometimes motorcycles. The car-free city is something that many city planners are seriously considering in relation to environmental threats and lack of fuel. They are looking at places like Venice, Marrakech or central Groningen. Perhaps the time has come to look at Dharavi. The diversity of activities that can be found within a ten-minute walk is wide ranging: schools, temples, mosques, shops and workplaces. The lack of infrastructure in things like water supplies, electricity, public transport, sanitation, healthcare and other services does not obstruct the intuition that Dharavi could be a more progressive city than the old one. Perhaps there is something to be learnt from Dharavi about the future of life without cars?

Perhaps there are also things to be learnt with regard to land use: in Dharavi, air-conditioned malls or parking lots occupy no space. The amounts of roads are at a minimum, meaning no pavements. There is no space that cools the houses and very few lifts. Instead, the people of Dharavi have developed systems of multifunctional surfaces, where private and public share, where work and recreation take place at different times or side by side. I can imagine that if Dharavi is allowed to continue to develop with some government support, it could be a city of the future. Dharavi has shown itself capable of organization and development, of diplomacy and ingenuity. In Dharavi one can sense hope and confidence for the possibilities of building, living and surviving.

When the American sociologist Emanuel Wallerstein proclaimed the death of Capitalism [in *After Liberalism – The End of the World as We Know It*, 1999], he also provokes us to imagine what would follow. When the great systems implode – what will germinate, emerge and rise up from the ashes?

Today the tendency over the world is clear when it comes to slum areas. Regardless of political or religious systems the middle class, politicians and people in positions of power have one and the same solution: demolition. But perhaps capitalist society has a lot to learn from informal structures of places like Dharavi, especially now that the developed world is finally becoming aware that its levels of consumption are totally unsustainable.

Perhaps the people who built Dharavi will observe this future. Perhaps it is the children of Dharavi who carry the answers as to what will come next. How one can live both with integrity and in a "global" manner. Maybe they are the ones who will show us how new democratic movements can be built; a neo-democracy where engagement can give us what we all are seeking: meaning, community and joy. In such an understanding of Dharavi, the fear of the urban poor can be transformed into a prospect that they are in fact the ones who will save us.   *ML*

Real World Dot Com

All over Colaba, a part of Mumbai with many hotels, you will find posters advertising "The Dharavi Slum Tour". A taxi driver notices our curiosity and steps forward to offer his services. As he speaks it is obvious that he is not representing any tourist company. Eloquently, he is just trying to make some extra money.

He tells us what to expect from the tour, if he would be our driver and guide: he will drive us around for two to three hours, showing us the misery of extreme poverty. But no one leaves the vehicle, no one can step out into this reality. The taxi driver says it is too dangerous, not even he would dare to walk around the slum.

Dharavi has a bad reputation. People still think it is a Mafia-run nest of drugs and prostitution that exists completely outside of the law. It is true that many people work and live in semi-legal or informal ways, but the boundaries between what is formal and informal, legal and illegal are not sharp but shifting. Products can be found on either side of these borderlines during different stages of production. And it is definitely not the people of Dharavi who draw the line and set the regulations about what is legal and illegal, formal and informal.

Everyone immediately understands the illusion of "realitytoursandtravel.com" that the reality in the slum is more real than the "ordinary" existence. How often do we not use the phrase "Welcome to reality" when we are confronted with misery, slum, war-zones and refugee camps … As if we believe that the conditions of catastrophes and disorder are more real, un-alienated, than everyday life. Today we seem to take Hegel's ideas concerning the Master-Slave dialectic, changed and developed by Marx, for granted; the slave knows more than his master as he stands closer to the realities of production. Not without nostalgia have these ideas become intertwined with thoughts that rural life, along with poverty and hardship, is more "real" and "true" than contemporary urban middle class culture. But the comparison halts as long as the question of where and what conditions are "the most real" remains unsolved.

The young taxi driver does not live in Mumbai himself. Just like many others working in the city he originally comes from a small village in the country. As he couldn't make a living there he has now been working in Mumbai as a taxi driver for over six years. Once or twice a year he visits his village. At night he sleeps in his car. His legs are hurting, as he cannot stretch out in the back seat of the car. If all this is true. Perhaps he too tries to ride on the wave of pity that he supposes motivates the slum tourists. Finally he admits that the tourist industry, himself included, makes a profit from the slum.   *JW*

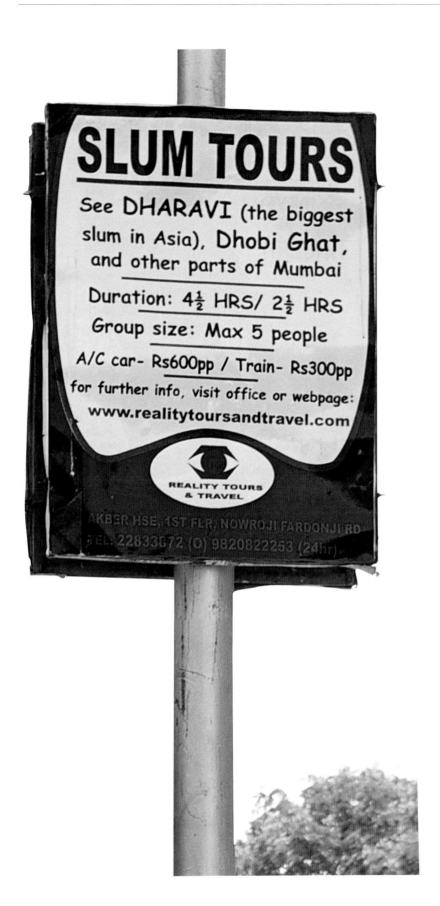

SLUM TOURS

See DHARAVI (the biggest slum in Asia), Dhobi Ghat, and other parts of Mumbai

Duration: 4½ HRS/ 2½ HRS

Group size: Max 5 people

A/C car- Rs600pp / Train- Rs300pp

for further info, visit office or webpage:
www.realitytoursandtravel.com

REALITY TOURS
& TRAVEL

AKBER HSE, 1ST FLR, NOWROJI FARDONJI RD
TEL: 22833672 (O) 9820822253 (24hr)

1:8

This poster in central Colaba lists the various tours and price options, including the length of the tours, air conditioning and different transport options.

The company's website seems to tell a slightly different story from the poster or taxi driver. "We think that Dharavi, the biggest slum in Asia, is one of the most interesting places to see in Mumbai. A few visitors such as Prince Charles and Bill Clinton have been to Dharavi, and it is by no means dangerous to go alone, but the beauty of Dharavi lies not on the main roads but in the small hidden alleys where thousands work and live in a number of small enterprises, where goats roam freely and where children play with carefree abandon."

According to the site, the tour's main objectives are to:

• Break down the negative image of Dharavi (and India's slums) and its residents.

• Highlight the small scale industries in the area.

• Bring people from different countries, races, religions and social classes together to increase understanding and empathy.

• Use tour funds to develop the Community and Education Centre.

• Give 80% of tour profits to NGOs working with Mumbai's poor communities.

A History of Dharavi

Seven social sins: politics without principles, wealth without work, pleasures without conscience, knowledge without character, commerce without morality, science without humanity and worship without sacrifice.

MOHANDAS GANDHI
YOUNG INDIA, *22 APRIL 1925*

Dharavi is an impossible place. It is impossible for almost 700,000 people to live on 1.75 square kilometres without an abundance of high-rises. It is also an unhealthy place with narrow alleys and overcrowded houses, where air and waterborne diseases are easily transmitted. It's swampy and wet with hazardous industries right next to where children play. Dharavi is an impossible place, a consequence of bad governance and sordid profiteering in a very ugly alliance.

Dharavi is a contradiction in terms. Everything said about Dharavi could be said differently, every understanding can also be understood in other ways. Speaking about Dharavi is like trying to talk with all of those voices at the same time. Impossible.

But even though it is impossible, people live here. In Dharavi the history of Mumbai is retold, as if it were a sharp piece of glass in the heart of Mumbai, reflecting and living the history of the city that surrounds it. What Mumbai has lost in the race for a global city branding can be found here in Dharavi, often referred to as a slum. It is closer to truth though, to call it an informal district where some areas are more established and developed, and others are standing without any infrastructural provisions at all and with very bad housing conditions. Many of Dharavi's inhabitants have been living here for three, four or even five generations. Others came yesterday.

BOMBAY, TRADE AND CONQUEST

Humanity has invented many ways to claim the right to land. In the globalization wave some five hundred years ago, the flag was the strongest statement. The first one there to hoist the flag won. This method of stating rights is used up to the present day. Consider the recent squabble for the raw materials presumed to be under the melting ice of the Arctic.

The document is for the individual what the flag is for the nation. Formal documentation is necessary for an individual to prove their right to inhabit land, even if they have been there for generations. There are many questions surrounding land ownership, rights, titles and tenure, especially in urban situations where masses of people with various interests share a limited space. Who has the right to what land, and on what terms? Who belongs to the city and who does the city belong to?

History is written by the ones who have both flags and documents. The documented history of what was first called Bombaim started when the Portuguese discovered a couple of islands with good and protected bays in the 1500s. The only people living there were the Koli fishermen. The Portuguese flag was hoisted without resistance and was in the air for a century, until the Bombay islands were given as a treaty to England through the marriage between Catherine of Braganza and Charles II in 1662.

With the map of Bombay (as they now called it) in their hands, the British Empire could hoist their flag over an unknown land of no major interest. Charles II persuaded the British East India Company to rent the islands for ten pounds of gold annually from 1668. There after followed almost two hundred years of conquest and ruling by an avaricious trading company. After the Sepoy uprising against the East India Company in 1857–58, the British Raj was appointed.

The British East India Company realized that Bombay had potential to become a commercial centre for global trade, with its protected harbours and international fairway. However, the population was very small and the Company had to attract important groups to the new town. With promises of free trade, freedom of religion and free settlement, Bombay grew quickly, from 10,000 in 1661 to 60,000 15 years later, a growth of about ten people per day. London by this time had 8 new inhabitants each day, and a total of 350,000.

In order to control politics and commercial interests, the British built a fortified city centre, concentrating all activity. After less than 100 years the city centre was over populated and when it burnt down in 1803, the city expanded to the north, outside the city walls. At this time Bombay island had half a million inhabitants. Within the walls, urban development had been monitored, but the outside settlement was free and unplanned.

All the new groups that came to Bombay contributed to its pluralistic profile, a diversity based on religion, ethnicity and craft. Different groups erected buildings necessary for their specific needs.

The promise of religious freedom led to different religious groups finding a safe haven in Bombay, but the boundaries between the various clusters were often clear. One could live in peace without much engagement with other societies except, perhaps, in the market places.

In the beginning of the 1800s the town was still located on Bombay island. The need for more space grew with the increasing population, and the land between the islands began to be filled. The hilltops of the islands were blown with dynamite and used as basic filling along with waste from industries and households. In 1845 all of the islands were connected into the peninsula called the Island City.

Bombay was divided into industrial enclaves ruled by different city patrons. The poor and workers' need for schools and healthcare were dependant on the goodwill of individuals. East India Company was founded on financial values and not on political vision. They were here to do business, not to build a society. As the city developed from a commercial town

National flag of India.
Adopted 22 July 1947.

National flag of Portugal.
Adopted 30 June 1911.

The flag of the British East India Company. The company's flag initially had the flag of England, the St George's Cross from the middle ages, in the canton.

Great Britain Union Flag, also known as the Union Jack. Introduced in 1606.

On 18 th of June 2007 Black flags where waved in Dharavi as a protest against the goverment's redevelopment project.

Bombay in the 18th century.

to a financial centre however, the East India Company realised the representative values of the city. When the British Raj came to power in 1858, they made an effort to transform the unstructured and what they saw as chaotic cityscape into a Victorian city symbolizing British law and order. But the transformation of an unplanned and crowded structure into a representative city of the world demanded a grand vision and a systematic change. And in the meantime more and more people were coming into the city.

There was no longer space for the craftsmen and small industries in the city centre, as their buildings were regarded as dirty and ugly in comparison to the new central skyline. The textile and leather industry was relocated in the less populated northern outskirts of the Island City.

During the mid 1800s the authorities built a modern city with developed infrastructure and a road system connecting the different parts. The most important transportation facility was the establishment of a railway system: the Central and the Western Railway. The city had a major economical boom during 1860s due to increased industrialization and became a leader on the global cotton market. When the Suez Canal opened in the 1869, the distance to Europe was shortened considerably, and Bombay's position as a global city was secured. Many new buildings were constructed, as the authorities tried to keep up with the 800,000 people now residing in Bombay, but the migration was massive and the shortage of housing became acute around the turn of the century.

20TH CENTURY BOMBAY

Bombay in the early 1900s.

When the Indian flag of freedom flew over the city in 1947, there were almost three million people living in Bombay. A large influx of people followed the division between India and Pakistan, and in a politically unstable time after independence, large areas of land were privatized. The urban sprawl grew and the Victorian city began to fade. By this time Island City was overpopulated, and the wealthy upper class had moved over to Salsette Island, across the Mahim River, giving the new northern parts a high status. The middle classes followed as rail and road connections made it possible to commute between home and work. Within a decade Bandra, Andheri, Malad and Borivali where incorporated into the development of Greater Bombay.

In those ten years the population grew by approximately 274 people per day, reaching a total of four million people in 1960. By that time 10% of the city's population were squatters in informal areas.

In 1960 Bombay also became the capital of the state of Maharashtra. Due to its increasing population the city faced tremendous pressure and the government enacted the Development Plan for Greater Bombay in 1964. The development plan included a standardization and a rationalization of construction laws. The Floor Spacing Index (FSI) was introduced giving all landowners standardized building regulations. Before the FSI, all building plans had to be assessed by use and location before they could be approved. With the FSI implementation many old sites were demolished in favour of more profitable residential high-rises. The original characteristics of Bombay city began to vanish and property prices soared. The increased expansion proceeded at an unstoppable rate.

Bandra Kurla Complex (BKC) just north of the Mithi river was established in the 1970s, a metaphor for India's financial and commercial capital, a financial district where many banks and other financial institutes have their main offices. It is a project that suggests the city's new identity as a prosperous financial capital, powerful enough to compete with China and Shanghai.

There are two excruciating extremes to be found on each side of the Mithi River, and it is the Bandra Kurla Complex on the north side and Dharavi on the south. The Mumbai Metropolitan Region Development Authority (MMRDA) has its office building in Bandra. This governmental authority is responsible for planning and developing civic infrastructure in Bombay Metropolitan Region, now following a master plan for the region until 2011. The plan follows what seems to be a global matrix for mega city branding. But the MMRDA has urgent and growing problems to deal with, far more demanding than ever before. During the 1960s the informal population was 10%, by 1980 the population had reached a total of eight million, of which 40% were living informally – and year 2000 the population had doubled again to 16 million (a daily growth of 1400 people) and now with 60% squatters. The number of migrants has decreased since the peak in the 60s, and the growth is mainly due to natural growth within the city. But as the city has grown so has the inequity. The slum dwellers share about 8% of the total urban land. The density rates for the city range from 27,000 people per square kilometre up to more than a 100,000. If Dharavi has the presumed 700,000 inhabitants, there are 400,000 on each square kilometre. The MMRDA in Bandra already has a new name for its poor neighbour Dharavi – Bandra Kurla South.

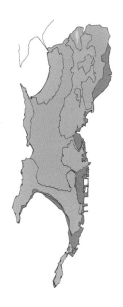

Bombay 1953.

DHARAVI

Dharavi is an informal slum area, one among thousands in the city of Mumbai, where more than 60% of the 19 million population of the city live. Four main factors make an urban area informal and it is the lack of (i) decent housing, (ii) sustainable drinking water and sanitation system, (iii) electricity and most of all (iv) secured tenure of land.

Without a secured tenure, the dwelling is considered illegal and the authorities have the right to evict the inhabitants, often without any permanent relocation solutions. Tenure, or title, is not secure for the people in Dharavi, but some are recognized by the government as "identified encroachers" which gives them some guarantees of compensation if they are relocated. Dharavi is a diverse district – mostly informal, with some formal parts, and some semi-informal. As the government has been forced to recognise Dharavi, it has provided some water taps and electricity, but it is generally not connected to the city's sewage systems. The building of a society starts underground where the water and sewage pipes are buried. Without this basic service, all building above ground is temporary, however solid.

But the definition of a city is not only the basic infrastructural functions and the systems – it is also the sum of the people, their identity, their lives and stories. Dharavi may be informal, impossible, hazardous and provisional but it is also a contemporary bearer of histories. All times are told and lived here. Deep, dark and colourful stories about the people who built and still build the city, who create and solve, develop and live. Their many voices recall a collective remembrance of the city, in a time of lost memory.

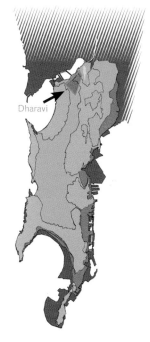

Bombay today. The map covers the southern part of greater Mumbai. (Expansion marked dark blue. Dharavi shadowed, blue outline.)

A HISTORY OF DHARAVI

Dharavi was founded on the very northern tip of Parel Island, long before Bombay. Inhabited by a Koli fishermen community, who had been fishing in Mahim Creek since time immemorial. Then the Portuguese came and hoisted a flag, built a small fort and a Jesuit church in Bandra on the opposite shore. Centuries passed and the Koli fished in the creek.

On a map from 1777, Dharavi is marked out as "a small town" between Sion and Mayham (Mahim).

In first half of the 1800s, during the reclamation of land, the Parel and Mahim islands were integrated in the new peninsula connecting all seven islands and became a part of the outskirts of the Island City. In this massive landscape manipulation, where the filling material here mostly consisted of waste from industries and households, the Mahim Creek ecosystem was disturbed. The biotope changed, and mangroves started to grow. The establishment of tanneries in Dharavi from 1887, finally killed the fish through chromium sulphide contamination and the Koli fishermen no longer had their traditional source of income. When Mahim Creek was overgrown and narrowed it became an extension of the Mithi River.

Once the Central and Western Railway lines were built, they created a border to this dirty and swampy area, to the north demarcated by the Mithi River. The old fishing village Dharavi gave its name to an area of 1.75 square kilometres, ignored by the authorities like a no-man's-land in a roundabout, and of no economical value.

All compromise is based on give and take, but there can be no give and take on fundamentals. Any compromise on mere fundamentals is a surrender. For it is all give and no take.

MAHATMA GANDHI

The first people to settle in Dharavi did so because the ground was still free and unregulated. It was a scrappy swamp far away from the city centre, and one had to build where it was possible. Undeveloped areas were used as a informal city dump, as the formal dump site was further north. Slowly the ground became more solid, even if parts where so wet that footbridges were still needed into the middle of the 1900s.

If we had a photo from the last half of the 1800s, taken from Mahim station at Central Railway, we would have seen a flat swampy landscape. To the far left in the picture, by the water, an old fishing village. Some small industrial buildings and residential houses without any visible structure could be seen in the middle where people would be occupied by outdoor work. There would be footbridges everywhere, and some dirt roads. We would see people selling on the street and dragging carts with goods. To the right in the picture, in the south, there would be smoke rising from the Kumbharwarda's kilns – the potters from Saurashtra in Gujarat, relocated by the authorities who did not want them in the expanding city centre any more. Further away, by the horizon at Girgaon, the high smokestacks of the textile mills, and even further south, one might catch a glimpse of the city's skyscapers.

In Dharavi, just like in Bombay at large, most people affiliated with those of similar heritage and language. The first migration to Bombay was from nearby areas, from Konkan and Gujarat. Some of them moved to Dharavi directly from their original homes, and others were relocated to Dharavi there from the city centre, as they were no longer wanted there. As the area grew denser, a pattern could be deciphered: language, religion, heritage and traditional production methods defined areas with floating and dynamic contours. Even if an area was dominated by one group, there were always other religions and languages close by. Different professions also settled together in nagars, and towards the end of the 1800s, large groups of Muslim tanners and leather workers from Tamil Nadu came to Dharavi from the more central parts of the city, and from Tamil Nadu directly to established the first tanneries. From Tamil Nadu also came chiki makers and embroiderers came from Uttar Pradesh. On a smaller scale, all different groups established similar enclaves which were to be found in central Bombay.

20TH CENTURY DHARAVI

During the first half of the 1900s, large groups of people came to Bombay from all over India. The city was still based on manufacture and in a need of cheap labourers. Many of them ended up in Dharavi for employment, creating an enormous need for housing. Most buildings served as both work and living quarters, with a production area on street level and the living quarters on top, a common split still used to this day.

Those who could afford to build more than what the family needed could make an extra income by subletting. Entrepreneurs could make a future for themselves by building, selling and controlling buildings. Dharavi became not only informal but also criminal in different ways. The Kolis who no longer could fish found an income by brewing and selling their traditional spirits. This soon slipped out of their hands and developed into an entire industry beyond the Koli community.

Liquor making became a way of earning daily bread for many people, but for the bootleggers and slum lords it became a means for power and capital. Various forms of shadowy activities moved into the narrow alleys and reached their peak during the 1980s when Dharavi was a centre for smuggling, brothels and gambling.

Even if crime was a problem, mostly for the local residents, the authorities chose to turn a blind eye to what was going on more than once, as many people could profit on the services and products provided by Dharavi.

During the late 1980s crime cumulated and the police had a tough job breaking this gang control, and stopping the illegal liquor production. Although the situation was under legal control, the broken structures turned into a time of economical and social confusion. An unexpected consequence was that a political extremism quickly established itself after the ruling gangs were gone. The Hindu nationalist party Shiv Sena gladly handled the confusion and the economical void left by the distilleries and their associated activities. Within a few years the party's orange flags could be seen in many places throughout Dharavi. This fuelled political tensions between Hindus and Muslims, who had been neighbours for so long. In 1992 rioting broke out. The conflict made deep wounds in Dharavi. Though this was not the only zone of the conflict, it was perhaps intensified by Dharavi's cramped conditions.

DHARAVI TODAY

The distinguishing mark of Dharavi has always been production. Some 80% of the people here have their income from production and only 20% work outside the area. In global comparison, most other informal areas have just the opposite situation and people usually

NAGARS AND CHAWLS

Nagar means town – eg Ahmednagar. But in the Dharavi context, it is a description for a certain geographical area which its residents feel they belong to. Postal or municipal authorities need not recognize it.

Chawls were one to three storey structures initially built by the British for migrant workers and their families. They had a common corridor and common toilets and an area of around 150 to 180 square feet.

CHIKI

Chiki is a special candy bar made with sesame seeds or peanuts in a toffee. Chiki has its origin in the state of Tamil Nadu but is now made throughout India and exported world wide, (see page 191).

work in the service sector. Mumbai is built on industries and manufacturing. But it has always been a global city and as the global economy has changed, Mumbai has followed. The industrial production has changed into commerce and service. After the closing of the textile mills and other industries, many workers had to go to the informal sector to find work, and it is here where an important link in the global production chain is found.

All kinds of products are made in Dharavi. The largest areas of production are the leather industry, food preparation, pottery and textile work, all of which were established at an early stage in Dharavi's development. Other crafts have followed such as goldsmiths, bakeries, printers and the production of all sorts of items for the global market.

The largest chain of production which involves the largest amount of people is the recycling industry. The recycled materials are mostly plastic-based. Oil and medical waste from hospitals are also recycled here. Everything that can be re-made, melted down or re-distributed is used. The goods are industrial waste, garbage emptied in the night by scavengers down in Island city, junk dumped in Dharavi or even exported waste from all over the world like chemical drums.

Recycling is an industry that turns over enormous amounts of money, and a large part of this industry has its end destination in export. A production chain might follow the following pattern: a woman has a small sewing machine that she sews new sacks with. The sacks are made from plastic weave, which she has bought from a basic plastic laundry. She sells them to a scavenger. The scavenger picks up plastic bottles from bins in the tourist areas at night. Once the sack is full it is re-sold to the recycling industry. After removing corks, caps and labels, workers press the bottles together into bundles and send them off to be cut into small pieces or pellets. The pellets are then sold on to China where they are refined. The material becomes filling in pillows, soft animals or fleece material. Products that stand a great probability of showing up in our local stores – Made in China.

The plastic might also be melted down in Dharavi and recast into all kinds of things such as the little piece of plastic in the collar of a new shirt – Made in Cambodia, Made in Turkey. Without exaggeration one might claim that we all own something that was made, at least in part, in Dharavi.

The products made in Dharavi are part of a global multi-billion dollar industry. In Mumbai as in many global cities it is the informal sector that is growing most rapidly, which of course means that formal economy and employment is increasing – tightly connected with the global economy.

Dharavi is an informal area, which means that the production in Dharavi to a large extent is informal. Although the production is informal, it is made out in the open air and hardly anyone is convicted for doing anything informal. It is not illegal – rather "alegal". As always, the weakest suffer the most: day labourers, women and children. The ones working with the heaviest jobs in hazardous, even lethal environments; the ones working thirteen, fourteen hours a day for food and shelter. Many are exposed to unhealthy products and waste in poorly ventilated rooms.

Can laws be transgressed if the authorities have not provided a system that makes it possible to follow them? How can one obey an environmental law, saying that you are not allowed to pour environmentally dangerous waste in the drainage, if there is no drainage to pour it in to? In a place like Dharavi, all kinds of legislations and rights become murky.

Who is protected by the legislations and who is outside? Who has the right and who does not? In essence these are questions about human rights. In a city like Mumbai, in a country like India there is a never ending asset of human beings. This inexhaustible resource of employees creates an employers market. The ones earning the most from Dharavi seldom live there, or in India.

Many of the people in Dharavi are the poorest of the poor, and some of them lack the most fundamental right of citizenship. Existing without documents means that you formally do not exist, that your children cannot be registered to go to school and the family cannot get ration cards. Registration costs money, often more than it should due to the amount of bribery surrounding the poor. But Dharavi also has stories of people who have come without anything but their bare hands and who have made a fortune. Unfortunately these success stories are often used to promote political policies where the individuals are depicted as creative entrepreneurs, whilst in reality they are left to fend for themselves, the responsibility of the government is at a minimum. There are in fact big differences in income in Dharavi, and a range from the poorest of the poor to the new rich live here. Many choose to stay, even if they might earn enough to move. It is matter of pride and identity as well as a matter of class, caste and stigmatization. For the major part, moving is not to be considered as long as the livelihood remains. Too many housing problems for the poor, or slum clearance projects, have been solved with relocation out on the outskirts of the city, far away from work and livelihoods, and where transportation often is ineffective and costly.

Dharavi is a tremendous proof of humankind's strength of will, ability, dignity and creativity. But it is also the place where the consequences of a reckless market and a short-sighted politics are brutally displayed. 2007 was the year when MMRDA finally took the decision to put Dharavi out on the global market. The land is so valuable today that profit from land sales will far exceed the total revenues being currently made in Dharavi. And of course it is the poorest who suffer the most. The ones who have a limited reliance on the society which does not recognise them as citizens. We all know how distressing it is to have vague or no idea about the future. How to support the family, where to live? To live in uncertainty is very painful.

Dharavi is under threat of turning in to Bandra Kurla South. Not very many of Mumbai's formal citizens are likely to notice when the bulldozers enter. It is a common scene. Houses are falling and rising everywhere. Old mills becomes residential areas, old residential areas become shopping centres. It is hard to see the city for all the houses, and it takes a lot of concentration and interest to catch the reflection in the window. Mumbai, the city that happened to be, it just became a global city from a fishing village. Nowhere can its distinctive character be reflected sharper than in the piece of glass at the centre of its origin. Mumbai was not planned from the beginning. But it is definitely not an ad hoc job to govern a huge city like the Mumbai of today. It needs an incredible amount of planning, responsible politics and inclusiveness. People's participation is a basic condition for a sustainable development.

Many different flags have flown in the sky above the city. People who have given themselves the right to land have hoisted flags and put the inhabitants under their own legislation. The people of Dharavi have never imposed any laws upon others, but now they have hoisted the black flags of Dharavi.

AE

All things appear and disappear because of the concurrence of causes and conditions. Nothing ever exists entirely alone; everything is in relation to everything else.

BUDDHA

1:9

1:10

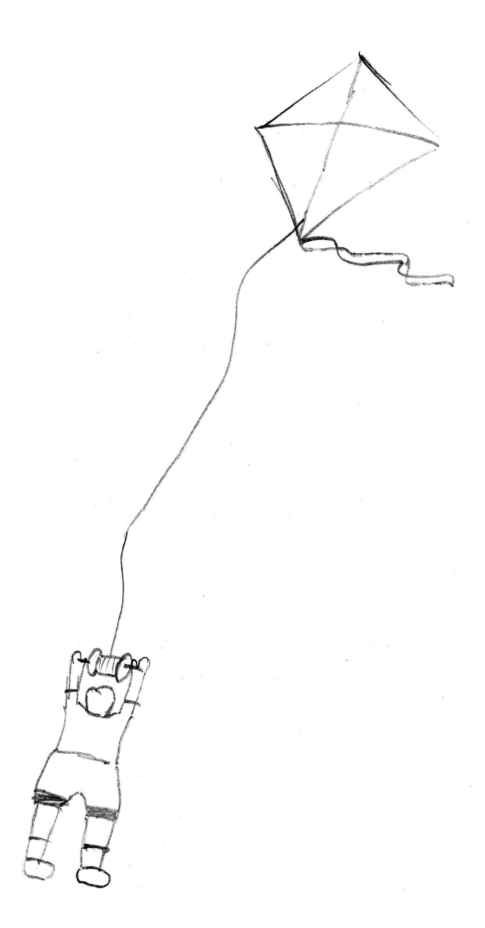

1:11

1:12

The Next Generation of Dharavi

People are born, raised, live their lives and die in Dharavi. But even if people seem rooted in Dharavi, many also have a profound relationship to their origins and to their relatives outside of Dharavi. When we asked the children of Poonawalla to draw their homes, many of them drew a house in the countryside, often with family members next to it. There were often mountains in the background, wells and fruit trees in a garden, images far away from the daily life in Dharavi. This gives a clue to the dualistic identity many families have: the life somewhere else and life in the city.

Family life is extremely congested in Dharavi. Neighbours and family members all encroach on an individual's privacy. Three generations often live under the same roof. Many families also sublet parts of their house to get an extra income. These crammed houses are often extended to the space outside. The borders between private and public as we know it in the middle class are not valid here. In Dharavi the public area lies directly outside the door. It is situated in all the in-between spaces where people meet: in the corridor between the flats, in alleys between houses, on streets and in marketplaces. Wherever there is an open space between the buildings in Dharavi there are children playing.

AE

1:9 (Page 52.) Central Railway with its tracks marking a boundary to Dharavi.

1:10 (Page 53.) Many of the people who used to live next to the railroad track have been relocated, making the railroad more efficient and life safer. The space between the tracks and people's homes has become a public area.

1:11 Drawing by Magesh Murugan.

1:12 Drawing by B Manoj.

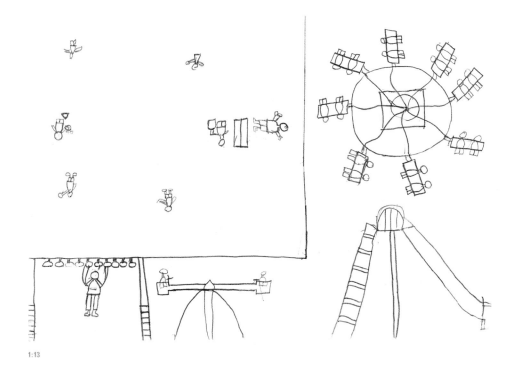

1:13

1:14

1:13 Drawing by Sofistic.

1:14 "Dream near my house" by Magesh Murugan.

1:15 Children from Poonawalla Street playing in the temple before drawing their homes..

CHAPTER 2:

POONAWALLA

– A WALK ON PV NEW CHAWL

City Planning

Today, most experts agree that one of the main problems in the world is global warming. Discharge from transportation plays a significant part in what we might call the "metabolism of the globe". Pollution from traffic occurs most within cities. In urban areas around the world billions of people are on the move every hour just to get to and from work.

"No one really lives where the work is." says Susannah Hagan, professor of environmental studies at The University of East London. Even though all cities contain both working and living spaces, this doesn't mean that the people who live in a place actually work in the same location, or vice versa.

From this perspective, Dharavi is an interesting and exceptional place. Here, people live most of their daily lives within the borders of Dharavi and yet are connected to the rest of the city by the two rail roads. This way of life – local, with your entire daily needs within walking distance and yet with the possibility to interact with the city around you – is an ideal situation for any city planner.

Dharavi is a place that has grown without any planners involved. Over the years it has become extremely dense. This kind of density does not create good living conditions – a lot more is needed: proper infrastructures such as water and sewage, access to privacy as well as to public spaces, and secure tenure – among other things. Yet, for future planners there is a lot to be learnt from the vernacular planning of Dharavi, for instance from the street of PV New Chawl.

PV New Chawl is one of the oldest streets in the neighbourhood. Once a market place, PV New Chawl today hosts family houses as well as public toilets, shops, workshops, a temple, a school, small offices, a bar, and other businesses. The street is approximately 500 metres long and is a good example of how daily life in Dharavi functions.

ML

2:1

PV New Chawl — the Street

PV New Chawl varies in width between 1.5 and 4.5m. The street widens at one point to accommodate the Ganhalhi Temple. Terraced buildings of one or two storeys line the length of the street. Behind the main chawl are smaller alleys referred to as A, B and C. These are more private streets between 1 – 2 metres wide and are only used for access to houses. The main Chawl includes housing, commercial, religious and social functions. There are no commercial frontages in the secondary alleys. There is one communal toilet block for the chawl at one end of the street. A covered channel for rainwater and grey water drainage runs the length of the street. A chawl office is situated half way along the street. The Chawl is too narrow for cars, only motorcycles, bicycles and carts have access to the street. Commercial premises are concentrated towards the larger road. Buildings looking like single family houses are often live/work spaces, sometimes shared by more than one family.

We saw that the street has an important social function with many families using the street as a living room. The street becomes more private as you move away from the larger road and foot traffic reduces. It seems that the street is divided into short sections as the scale and use of buildings changes, with noticable changes in character. The use of the street and the semi-private terraces by residents means that the street is always occupied. This complex relationship between public and private space in PV New Chawl is of special interest when looking at the functional requirements of housing in Dharavi.

ML

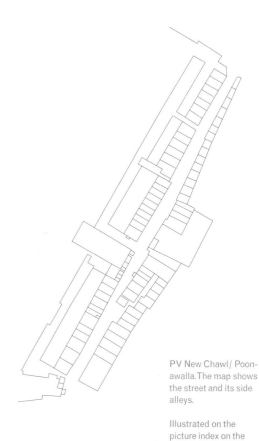

PV New Chawl / Poonawalla. The map shows the street and its side alleys.

Illustrated on the picture index on the right and the following pages is the walk up and down the busy PV New Chawl. The street is barely 110 metres long with some 60 houses.

PUBLIC TOILETS

PUBLIC TOILETS   HOUSEHOLD WASTE TIP

SHOP   HOUSE

HOUSE   HOUSE

HOUSE   HOUSE

HOUSE MAGESH   HOUSE MANAJ AKANSHA

HOUSE SACHIN   SABARI STORES / PHONE / HOUSE

HOUSE   HOUSE

HOUSE   IDLI DOSA CAFE / HOUSE

HOUSE R.S. PILLAI   HOUSE

IDLI DOSA CAFE / HOUSE   HOUSE

HOUSE   HOUSE

NURSERY / HOUSE   HOUSE SARAN

HOUSE SHAKTI MARI   HOUSE KISHAN

KKAMINAR TEMPLE   HOUSE R. BHAGYALAXMI

HOUSE S. RAMESH   MODERN ARTS GRAPHIC DESIGN / HOUSE

HOUSE S. SUBRAMANIAN   HOUSE GANESH

HOUSE RAM   IRONING SERVICE / HOUSE SUKU KUMAR

HOUSE REVATHI   HOUSE

HOUSE   RAHAT BAKERY

HOUSE   RAHAT BAKERY SHOP

HOUSE   HOUSE

HOUSE   HOUSE

PCO TELEPHONE AND INTERNET SHOP   HOUSE

CHAWL OFFICE / SOCIAL CENTRE   HOUSE A. RURBAN ASIR

ROHINI COMMUNICATION, TELEPHONE SERVICE   BHAGYA PHOTOS

IRONING SERVICE   GANHALHI TEMPLE (LENTIL FOODSTALL ON STEPS)

BARBER   T-SHIRT PRINTER

HOUSE A. JAYKUMAR   HOUSE

HOUSE   HANUMAN "MARUTI" TEMPLE

HOUSE   STORE (OWNED BY SADASHIVA WINESHOP)

KGN WOODLIGHT, IRONMONGER   PRIYA BEAUTY PARLOUR

GOUTOM STORES, FOOD SHOP   MANGO SWEETS SUPPLIER

SEWING SERVICE   GENERAL GOODS SHOP

SADASHIVA WINESHOP, BAR   HOUSE

SHREE BALAJL JEWELLERS   VEEKAY COMPUTERS (CASINO)

NK MHAVARKAR, TAILOR   KRISHMANADA HOTEL

HOUSE

GERSHAH, FOORD AND BATHROOM SHOP

NEELAM, FOODSHOP

TATA INDICOM CORNER TV REPAIR

PJ POOJA JEWELLERS / HOUSE

HOUSE

NEW SHIVAM JEWELLERS

MAHALAXMI BAKERY, GENERAL STORE

LOTTERY SHOP (EVENING ONLY)

SEA ROCK CHEMIST

2:2   Coming from the marketplace you can turn left
by the druggist and find yourself on Poonawalla.

2:3   At the beginning of the street, there are shops and workshops on both sides. A jeweller, a shop with telecom and electronic equipment and a small bar on the left-hand side. On the right side there are various manufacturers: a repair shop, a sweet maker, a computer business and a hostel.

2:4   Further down the street, the bakery is busy 24 hours a day. Bicycles
take the bread to both local shops and the rest of Mumbai.

2:5   In this part of the street, life is more quiet. The houses are usually two stories and sometimes they host one family on the ground floor, another one upstairs. Poonawalla is one of Dharavi's oldest streets and was once a market street. Today the street is densely populated and serves different purposes: a passage between different areas, a shopping street and a place where travelling salesmen can offer their goods to the local residents.

The street is also a continuation of the homes along Poonawalla. Food is sold on the street, and clothes can be sewn and repaired in the shade, whilst keeping an eye on the children. The street is also a public space for playing and exchanging information between residents and those passing by.

2:6   The houses have one or two floors, in certain cases there might even be a third. Many forms of leases exist here: from an ownership where the family have papers concerning their right to possession, through to letting and subletting contracts. However, the contracts are informal and not always legally binding. On the left-hand side we see the residents Gomn, Akansha, Priya and Laxmi. Laxmi, wearing a green sari, is busy talking to her neighbour.

2:7   The toilets are at one end of the street. They have been built through common funding via a local organization. The street continues and branches off into alleys and new streets.

2:8   If you turn around and walk back, you can walk into "rush hour traffic". The market place is now at the far end of this street.

1:9   Afternoon relaxation at Poonawalla.

2:10   The closer one gets to the market and the end of
Poonawalla, the more shops there are by the road.

2:11   At the end of the street there is an alley that turns
off to the right, leading to a narrower, parallel alley.

2:12   In the market street, the tempo is different and the sound level higher. Here
the salesmen try to be heard over the motorcycles. There is a Friday afternoon
liveliness.

Measuring the Life of a Street

This conversation took place in Stockholm following a two week visit to Dharavi. Jake Ford is a landscape architect, Jonas Jernberg an architect and Jonatan Habib Engqvist a writer and philosopher.

JF, JJ and JHE worked collaboratively during the visit to Dharavi in March 2005, having pre-defined a methodology in order to document a place – the simple task of measuring a street. This was a seemingly manageable scale, necessitated by the short length of our stay and our lack of knowledge of the place. Parallel to our study we would also attempt to obtain as many official plans of the area as we could find.

We had visited Dharavi together prior to the visit in 2005 but we had only seen the slum from the roof of an adjacent high-rise building. Therefore we had little idea of the place on ground level, rather a familiar image of the slum as a continuous field of corrugated tin roofs.

Before going to Dharavi there was already an idea that by concentrating on the documentation of the physical structure, we would in some way formalise an informal part of the city. We also hoped that the naïve study would allow us to experience and comprehensively document a place in detail rather than attempting a general overview of Dharavi as a whole.

The conversation is an attempt to consolidate the huge amount of varied information and thoughts into a cohesive statement about our experience. What had been seen and what can be learned from the field trip as well as the application of a very simple objective, to measure a street.

The conversation attempts to record our personal experiences from Dharavi as well as to discuss the successes, failures and relevance of the methodology we employed.

JAKE FORD: This started with a study focusing on relationships between formal and informal architecture and economy.

JONAS JERNBERG: Or rather a documentation of that relationship, based on a case study of Dharavi.

JF: Well to begin with Dharavi was not much more than a name to us, we had been there before but we didn't know very much about it. So we started to research and find as much information as possible about Dharavi.

JONATAN HABIB ENGQVIST: Quite soon we realized that most of the information we found about the place seemed to come from people who did not actually live there, and I guess that we are adding ourselves to that list.

JF: It is mostly described in terms of "the biggest slum in Asia" or as a "seething mass of activity, deprivation and commerce".

JJ: Also given the resistance towards letting us into the area in our prior visit, which could be interpreted with regard to potential violence. We had read about the communal riots in Dharavi in 1992–93 and our impression was that it could be a challenge just to work there.

JJ: Big things, very dangerous.

JHE: Above all we had a very abstract image of the place and perhaps that is why we decided to formulate our own task very clearly, taking care to prepare ourselves, or rather our project very systematically. You could say that we had no idea as to where we were going but a pretty clear idea of what we would do when we got there.

JF: It was a form of panic almost, to have a plan – or structure to start off with.

JHE: Why is that? Why was it so important to have a plan more or less fixed to begin with?

JF: I think that partly has to do with our professional background. As architects and academics, we are used to having some sort of brief or primary study to discuss before beginning a project, but I think more importantly because we did not have so much time there.

JJ: Yes, I think it had to do with the fact that time was so limited and the task was in a way impossible.

JF: As you suggested earlier, one could compare it to, say documenting Stockholm in two weeks. I mean, one million people – how should one go about that? How do you do it and more importantly – what story do you choose to tell?

JJ: Another source of inspiration at the time was a book that you had read that gave an interesting view on documentation which we thought could be used in this project.

JHE: Species of Spaces.

JF: Yes, Georges Perec. It is a documentation of scales, macro- and micro- perspectives on the commonplace; like documenting a bed, a room, house or a street. I was looking for models to use for documenting an unknown place. Also the idea of documenting the everyday, as I thought we could easily get distracted or overwhelmed by the "spectacular".

JJ: Knowing what to do there also made us relax. It felt easier for us, more secure, but it was also a kind of test. We wanted to see if we could follow this idea through the whole process even though we were not sure what to expect once we got there.

JF: There was a physical dimension in this too. We understood at quite an early stage that we couldn't look at Dharavi as a whole. If we wanted something worthwhile we would have to change scale and focus on a street or even a section of a street. We decided that from our perspective, a single street would serve as a kind of example of what the area might contain, which of course is a choice that could be criticized as naïve. But this was the decision we took, it felt like the honest thing to do and we stuck to it through the whole process.

JHE: Without actually knowing anything about what a street might look like structurally in Dharavi. It is indeed quite an assumption that one could find a street that would represent an area with a million inhabitants, again – compare it with Stockholm. Which street would you choose?

As we were saying earlier, I think the choice was made on a rather vague understanding of the area that we were going to visit. Apart from what we had read, the trip to Calcutta and a rooftop view from a high-rise in the outskirts of Dharavi in 2004, we had very little knowledge of the place we were going to document.

JF: Another important thing about the place we did choose – PV New Chawl – is that there were quite a lot of us in the larger group who spontaneously liked it and wanted to work with it. Personally, I think that this has to do with our eurocentric perspective: it was quaint, there were families living and working there, children on their way to school and people just getting on with their lives.

JJ: Yes, the first impression was, I guess, romantic and it did seem like a well-ordered and idyllic village community. It felt safe.

JHE: Perhaps it was a question of recognition?

JF: It was a well established and functioning area. Families had been living there for generations. It was like the ultimate informal society. So, yes, there was a sort of romantic recognition at play there.

JJ: Paradoxically, we seemed to choose an area that we experienced as a kind of post-slum. In the sense that it was not a slum any more because it did not feel slummy according to our almost clichéd idea of a slum. In fact we suspected that this area could be based on one of the fishing villages that pre-date Dharavi. It felt very much like a village street.

JHE: Another interesting thing that happened when we had picked a spot and wanted to measure out "our" street is that we discovered that there was in fact not a street. Instead of a street, we found it was a chawl and we spent a lot of our time trying to figure out what a chawl is.

JF: Actually, I am not really sure if we know what a chawl is. I know it is a form of European import, something like a tenement and that it has to do with houses that define a zone or a stretch of road. When we asked people where the chawl started and ended, we got different answers.

JHE: The physical boundaries of the chawl seemed to vary.

JF: A lot of the things that we looked at based on our plan seemed to have this character.

JJ: We had the idea of taking photographs, measuring, taking notes in order to thoroughly document this area, but things kept happening that would not fit the model. For example we had written down all the house-numbers but then it turned out that the numbers we were using were a completely different system. The numbers on the houses in Dharavi did not refer to the order of the houses along a horizontal line, as they would do in Europe. Instead they referred to electricity supply and water distribution.

JF: Doctors visits and things like that could be organizational principles, which is quite different from the systematic grid thinking that we were into.

But we did get a plan of the area from Jockin (image no. 2:13). This plan was more or less, but not entirely, correct. We measured every millimetre and yet we now know that our map is also inaccurate. Actually I think it is a good thing. Certainly good to acknowledge.

It took two weeks of hard work and still we had to cheat in order to make it work out. So the map we got was incorrect, we measured every inch and our map is also incorrect.

JHE: I was thinking that this might have to do with perspective. When we were in India, I thought a bit about orientation in the city. We have a sort of habitual bird's-eye perspective with us, and I do not think that this is an occupational hazard, at least not entirely. Our starting point is often a vertical interpretation of the space we are in, based on maps, etc. And if a stranger shows up we generally tend to use that model. Perhaps we will draw up a map and say "you are at this point and should be moving toward that point, this line represents the shortest route," all from this from a bird's-eye perspective. However, in the short periods of time that we have been in Mumbai, I experienced that practically all instructions and descriptions of spatial orientation where horizontal. Directions were taken and given by means of landmarks, perhaps as a more relational method of describing space. At times I could even interpret this relational space as series of habitual routes. You could ask two different people for directions and one of them would direct you to the left, actually you are more likely to be led to where you are going, and the other to the right. Both routes are going to get you to where you are going, but the two individuals you have asked have different habitual patterns or routes. Sure, phenomenologically we move around the city like that too, but in this case it is more obviously not only the primary space experience but space is also communicated in that way.

JF: That way the city becomes more of a continuous landscape. Instead of grids or recognizable city patterns we have a form of flowing urban space.

JJ: Exactly. And in that way it can never be finished, never a static or finite space.

JF: I experienced something similar when I was in Kampala. People did not move between the houses on a street. It was more of a movement on a surface. Dharavi was of course more contested but I recognised this surface-movement.

JHE: In Mumbai an address, or even a postal address would be given in a similar fashion, "behind the cinema, next to the temple in this or that district", and something similar also came to my mind when we were talking about the concept of the chawl. It is difficult to understand how it is defined physically, since it does not seem to be limited by the physical buildings, perhaps officially, but not the way we understood it on location. Somehow buildings adjacent to what we might call a street were included for example. I could find it easier to comprehend this if it could be understood in terms of relationships. People, who move within the area, expand their family-domains so to speak; will also be included in the chawl that they stem from. Its organizational principle being not dictated from above, but rather from within. Something like a relational cluster.

JF: I also understood it as having to do with identity, or cultural ancestry. Most of the people on PV New Chawl seemed to be Tamil and had a common group identity.

JHE: Another factor is the use of houses, because most of them serve multiple purposes. A house is not just living quarters occupied by one family and the program is often a lot more complex than a simple live/work space.

JF: So there are several parallel relationships going on?

JJ: Well, we listed all the different activities on PV New Chawl and found so many different things going on in this limited space: lottery, food shops, casino, temples, jewellers, tailors. This enormous variation and density of functions is amazing. It was like a city within the city, with the same pressure, or pulse as a metropolitan area.

JF: Simultaneously everybody seems to know everybody.

JJ: But it is important to note that this is not a satellite city and cannot be compared to one. Dharavi is special because it is so central, giving it energy and intensifying it.

JHE: Which also shows how delicate the situation is. You could say that every plan for this area of one million potential voters is a form of heart surgery on the city of Mumbai. The municipality has to be aware of this. The difficulty in getting hold of plans is most probably not only a sign of a topological problem, but also a political one – mainly due to that fact that it is a central location. I mean, just defining land is a political statement here, let alone deciding who owns it.

JJ: During this whole process, we have met a lot of different groups with various interests and agendas in Dharavi and of course we were and are also one of these groups. Everyone has some kind of stake in Dharavi, be it SPARC, The Slum Development Authority or academic tourists like us. Trying to understand this part was perhaps even more delicate than trying to grasp the physical complexities of Dharavi.

JHE: I think we are pretty naïve too. We are generally gullible and pretty bad at interpreting all the layers that are behind each "official" statement – what does so and so actually want? What is not being said here? And so on. What does the same statement mean in different contexts?

JF: I think that is an unsolvable task for us, considering the complexity and the time at hand. But another thing that you talked about a lot that also relates to these limitations is the idea of boundaries. I remember that when we first came to Dharavi there were a lot of presumptions based on the information that we had gathered in our research. The idea of the largest slum in Asia implied a lot of respect and perhaps also a little fear. When we were going to enter the area for the first time, we arrived in this air-conditioned jeep and were given an introduction in the SPARC office just on the border to the slum. In fact I remember that there was a physical wall there, marking out the boundary. We were briefed on things like moving in groups so that we wouldn't intrude too much and so on.

JHE: In fact on our first trip we never went into the area for these very reasons. Our first image of Dharavi was the bird's-eye view of tin roofs and the yard of a tannery. The idea of the slum, or the image of the image.

JJ: But then we crossed the boundary and walked into the area we came to PV New Chawl. When we had been there for several days in a row the situation was completely different. We found the same thing on the other side of that boundary and the boundary did not exist any more. The people who lived there are the same people you would find here, or anywhere for that matter, they are just living within different physical parameters.

JHE: We were quite critical to a lot of things in SPARC's housing project after our first visit almost three years ago and there where a lot of things that we had to not only confront but also re-evaluate.

The premise for this first criticism was, if I remember correctly that people used to living in a village-like environment, socializing and living as it where "horizontally" would not only object to, but in fact be radically effected by a transition into a vertical living situation as in the case of a multi-storey buildings.

This critique is, when seen from a broader perspective – not only extremely reductive, and taken the contestation and sanitation problems – ridiculous. It shows how blind

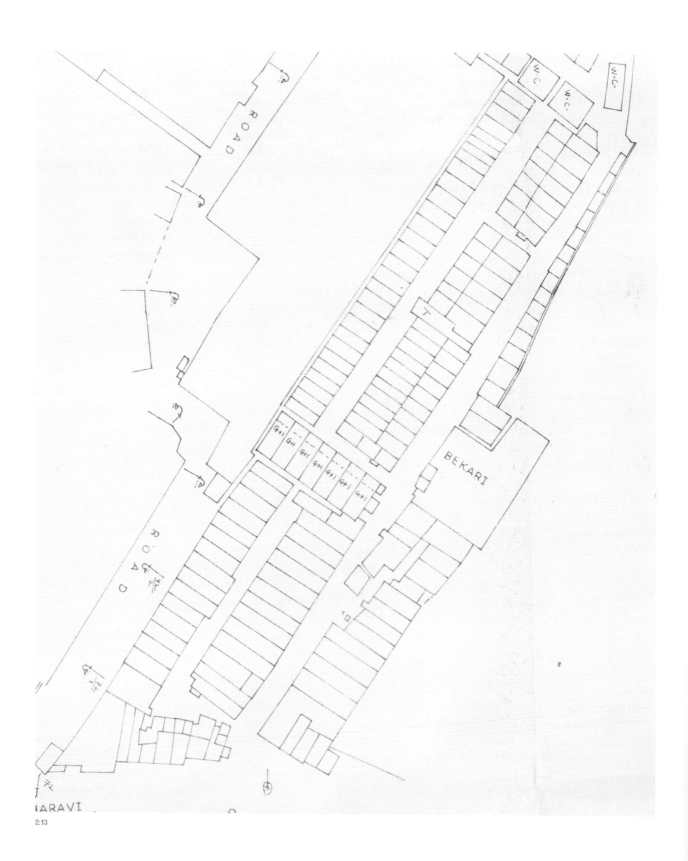

2:13   Detail of survey by
       SPARC showing
       PV New Chawl.
       Scale 1:500

2:14   Our survey of
       PV New Chawl.
       Scale 1:500

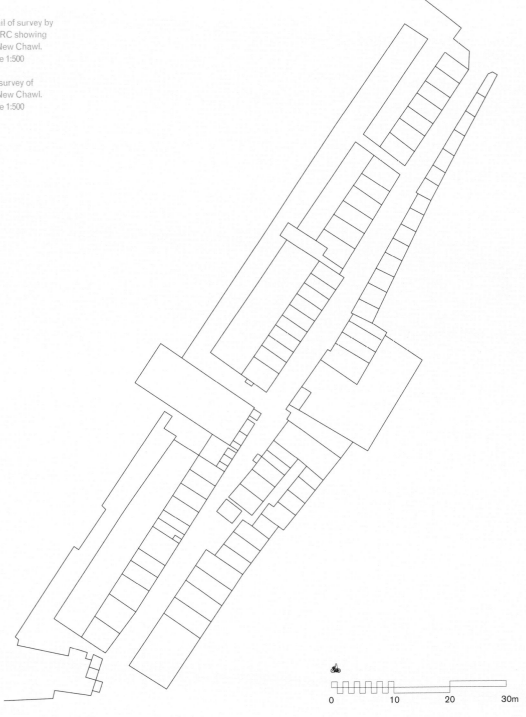

0   10   20   30m

we were to the nature of boundaries, the real architectural problems of Dharavi and what happens when this misunderstanding is combined with a certain strand of not only romanticizing the situation but also making general assumptions about what the slum dwellers really want.

More importantly it shows how we totally misunderstood, not only the inhabitants of Dharavi's problems and needs but also their relationship to space, and indeed our own. Most of the tenants seemed to be more than satisfied with their new situation. When asked about the transition from a shack in one of the better chawls of Dharavi to the sixth floor of a high-rise, one woman exclaimed, "Of course this has affected my social life – now I can have one! Living at this height makes me feel rich, now friends and relatives come to visit us." She could now invite people over, without having to be ashamed, and I think that we really missed out on that very fundamental problem in our first criticism. I think a lot of this was certainly due to our vertical vantage point, standing on that roof looking down on the corrugated iron landscape below.

JJ: Of course there are better or worse solutions to these problems, but if we look at it from a planning perspective, regardless of romanticizing or not, it is impossible to say that socially pv New Chawl is a bad environment.

JHE: And you're right – what I mean is rather the opposite – we assumed that the transition of moving from the chawl and into a tall building would be something negative, where in fact there basically is a very practical problem of resources. If you could choose, wouldn't you want a water closet? Anyhow, it is partly a question of finding solutions to very elementary problems, but I do not think that is my main issue here. If we look at ourselves or if we just refer to architecture. I think that there were certain things that got us going that were more about architectural utopias than the physical problems of the area, like sanitation.

JJ: No, I really don't agree with your description here. The problem with the high-rise buildings is something different. It has to do with the lack of ideas for the space in-between the buildings, how they communicate with each other, the streets. It's simply a bunch of buildings and they just stand there without a context of their own, whereas one might do Dharavi more justice if it were understood as a whole context or series of typologies.

JF: It is about the informal village structure that the slum builds on. Taking an available area of five metres and building something there or perhaps building something in-between two existing houses. This is fine, but there is no original organizing principle or structure at play other than this and things are solved afterwards – often very creatively. However, when SPARC housing is presented as an alternative, taking the chawl structure and moving it into a multi-storey building they seem to have a lot of good ideas about live/work accommodation – and I do think that this is a good thing – the buildings are seen as individual plots. That's it. There is no real planning perspective. Which of course also is, given the situation, understandable. When they are given a plot, they say, "Okay, let's just build as high as we can, filling the plot, so that as many people as possible can be re-housed". But what one can expect from that logic is a lot of the same problems that can be found in the chawl only scaled up.

JJ: You mean similar to some of the social problems that we have experienced in European cities?

JF: I don't know, I was just thinking structurally. The fact that they did not talk at all about public space, relationships within the urban spaces and streets. There may be larger structural plans for building but there was no discussion about this when we were there. So in the existing situation and in the SPARC projects that we looked at, it was more a question of if there was land available to build on or not. But it is interesting that SPARC act as "developer", demanding maximum densities. Then we also looked at the Slum Rehabilitation Authority (SRA) and their plans, which are on a completely different scale. Or at least the vision that they presented to us about what they saw as the possibilities for the area.

JJ: They basically want to transform the whole area, completely.

In order to say anything about this, I think that we have to relate these two different visions or master plans to each other.

JHE: And we did get to see a general master plan from the municipality, which means that we do know something about that. Because this is also a question: what we know or don't know and what we are relating to when we are talking.

JF: Sure, we do not know that much about the master plan for Dharavi. We only know what we have been shown, and what they actually showed us was in fact not that much. Something like four or five zones labelled A, B, C, D, one dedicated to sports, one to industry etc. When we came back from the meeting and were talking to some of the others from the Dharavi group, many of them were really upset when we mentioned a jogging-track from the SRA proposal. I think it was because the general impression was that the municipality just wanted to clean up and sell off the land. The SRA presented a global tender that was going out to developers. But honestly we need to know so much more before we can make any statements about this what so ever. What can we scientifically say? What do we actually know?

JHE: Okay, let us just try to be very straight about it. What happened when we went to Dharavi? Let us just start there. We went there. Then we got out our rulers and started measuring.

JF: And everybody asked us what we were doing.

JJ: Lots of people found it very amusing.

JF: Some people seemed very suspicious but I never felt any kind of hostility – a lot of questioning though. We tried to explain what we were doing and through our measuring we came into contact with most people that lived on the chawl.

That is actually where the interesting things happened – in that meeting. You could say that our process helped us to get there, to that meeting; our process and the fact that we had pre-defined it. The process became the tool.

JHE: I would like to try my idea of relational space again. Would you agree that the physical space became an excuse to investigate a relational space? Or to put it differently: even if the physical space was the original object of interest, the most interesting results were to be found within relational space?

JF: Well perhaps one could see physical space as a kind of hub. For example we got to know this man called Mani who was a graphic designer and had his office on the first floor of a house on PV New Chawl. His mother still lived there on the ground floor but he had moved out if I remember correctly.

JF: It was one of those coincidences. Because at that time we had the idea that our project for this book would be a documentation of how we went about making this book in Dharavi and then getting it made there. And since this was in the back of our minds, it seemed like it would be a really good thing if we could find people who had connections or worked with printing in different ways. I still find it fascinating that we chose a more or less random spot and met somebody who happened to be a graphic designer who worked in this hidden office that you got to by climbing a ladder. I also think it shows something about our prejudices – graphic designers and slums seem worlds apart in our preconceptions.

JJ: According to the mediated image, slum inhabitants are primarily if not potential criminals then at least poor souls that need guidance, and the least we can do with this project is to say that this is not the case. Dharavi is an extremely productive and creative space that definitely plays an important part not only in the bigger city but also in many formal economic structures.

JHE: It is really the heart of the city of Mumbai. Look at the enormous catering industry, the laundry, I mean all kinds of basic services are run from or through Dharavi. This example also shows the mix of high and low tech.

JJ: Mani took us to several different printers in the area, and we found everything from old techniques like letterpress to the absolutely latest digital machines that would print enormous Bollywood billboards and banners. These could be something like 20 metres wide.

JF: I think it is quite a good example, because there have been lots of discussions about the different industries that we saw, industries that are particular to Dharavi and that the area is famous for. When we looked at the printing industry as another one of those industries, one not associated with slums, we could see the different printers producing ads and signs for other local industries as well as for international corporations. There are printing presses from Germany that are 100 years old and also the absolute latest stuff, mostly being used in a small-scale cottage industry. This gave us an interesting insight of Dharavi that we would not have got otherwise, and I think it was primarily because we had this plan to find people working within book printing. So as you were saying about this relationship between physical and relational space – there was this relational-chain that started with Mani, where we came into contact with all these other people.

JHE: In this case, it is not only a question of relationships between places, that is, not only relations between topological points, but rather relationships between pockets: pockets of space. Perhaps even pockets of time. And in order to find ones way in a structure consisting of relationships between spatial and temporal pockets one needs completely different tools than those used from the vantage point of a bird's-eye view. Yet this is precisely what we are publishing here! It's a great paradox isn't it? We are still trying to represent this experience in the form of these very schematic, traditional sections and diagrams.

JF: But there are also reasons why we have chosen to present it like this. We talked about things like not publishing photographic images for example, because you do not need to know the colours of a specific wall when looking at structural aspects of a place. And yet the standardized or reduced drawings can still give you an idea of the physical space.

JJ: You might say it is an attempt to make an objective, or at least a less subjective documentation, that as you said, does not show what material is used or that we are dealing a slum area. It is just a place that has certain physical attributes, scales and relationships. That is what we were interested in.

JF: If you read "wine shop and bar" for example, it could be anywhere – a street in most cities. The map becomes a collection of different activities. And for us it started to become more interesting.

JHE: So maybe we could say that it is about formalizing the informal. Formalizing the informal architecture of slums in order to get some kind of formal recognition.

JF: It was important from the start as I recall to do something very straight-forward and simple, draw something where anybody could recognise it without necessarily seeing it as a slum, since a slum often becomes an object in itself.

But as we realized at an early stage, the difference between what we found on one side of the boundary and the other was in fact not that big – the main difference perhaps being that of land ownership.

JJ: And that everything in the slum is not just a repetition of the same. There is an enormous variety of environments: rich people, people who worked on oil-platforms, people living in villas with their own garden, and then there were those who lived in shacks where the streets were no more than 50 centimetres wide.

JF: So we had to take a decision early on as to which

slum to record. Is it the life of those on the pipeline? Or is it those living by the train track? – Is this the true Dharavi, or should we look at this area that has developed over many years and become something more? We picked a spot where there was a lot of variation of activities, but I guess this is one of many possible pictures.

JJ: Dharavi is all of this. We chose a very diverse area that has a huge variety within it but you cannot say that one aspect of it is more slum than another. One can only state that these are different environments.

JHE: Maybe it is not a quantitative question either. Perhaps we are getting back to what we were talking about in the beginning again, namely boundaries.

If a boundary is not seen as a limit or as the enclosing of a territory but rather as an opening, the boundary becomes something from which something else can come forth. We can say that we have chosen a certain space to study, but this does not necessarily imply that our limitations or boundaries will close or restrict Dharavi to that space. Instead perhaps other chawls and environments might precede. Hopefully one could also see aspects of not only other informal environments but also of our own environment. A number of different typologies can be made visible through the chawl structure that we have chosen, they can be related to each other, and in this case there is a greater possibility to make that comparison than in the case of, say a 50 centimetre wide alley.

JF: Just to walk in there and start measuring would not be possible, emotionally as well as physically. This is also an attempt from our point of view to work with documentation without evaluating or judging to much. Basically transcribing a physical milieu.

JHE: Did we succeed? Or rather, in what way did we and did we not succeed with regard to the original ambition to find a more neutral model of description as it were? Have we altered anything during the process?

JF: Of course we are constantly evaluating things and making judgements in different ways. It is a tricky thing and there are always so many sides to each story. All the immediate reactions to radical plans for the development of the area, that would transform Dharavi into something entirely different for example. These reactions are maybe hasty because Dharavi is constantly transforming itself, and sometimes in radical ways. The case of the printing industry is a relatively innocent example – in forty years time most of the older printing presses will probably be out of use, regardless of external pressure. Hopefully they will be gone, because a lot of them are also exploiting people under slave-like conditions. Or take the industries we saw where people were working with hazardous chemicals – none of those who react strongly against the master plan will condone that, and yet they are in some way against the will to make a radical change without really offering a different solution to these problems. Of course it is important to criticise decisions being taken in an entirely top-down manner. But you can't claim that everything should stay the way it is. The slum is in constant transformation as is the city of Mumbai.

JHE: The specific issues you are addressing can perhaps be clarified if you think about Dharavi as a part of Mumbai, and then compare it with other central areas of Mumbai, where for various political reasons, the rent cannot cover the costs of keeping the buildings and therefore does not change. It does not change because it cannot change until it simply deteriorates. So large areas are purposefully left to deteriorate so that they can be entirely restructured.

JF: I don't quite understand what you are getting at.

JHE: I was just thinking about the system where people are paying the same rent as they were when they first moved in to a flat. Actually the rent can even be inherited. So someone is paying the same price for a four-bedroom art-deco apartment on the waterfront as someone else might pay for a shack in Dharavi.

In central parts of Mumbai it is not a question of even wanting the same but better. It is rather just waiting until things fall apart enough so that you can tear it down and build something else on that plot instead. Dharavi is also a central part of Mumbai, but you cannot sit around and wait for the slum to fall apart by itself because the slum will not fall apart. It is the slum's nature to constantly renew itself. It works with a diametrically different mechanism. PV New Chawl has undergone a number of renewals to get what it is today.

So when you were talking about the resistance toward transformation, and this idea of wanting the same but different, I was thinking that it might look different if one could see it from that horizon.

JF: Well it is an interesting and peculiar relationship you are describing, especially in economical terms. The slum is perhaps seen as a place where it still is possible to do something.

JJ: Another important thing about that from our perspective is that we in a way perceived Dharavi as a democratic structure in the sense that it is a self-structuring organism. So when we hear about plans to tear it down, or the large scale plans for transformation, we interpret these as a threat to the current generative structure of the space. Moreover, we seem to interpret the situation in such a way that there is no space for negotiations, no middle way. We have a mega-city with two extreme positions simultaneously – on the one hand an extremely progressive high-tech logic, and on the other this village structure right in the city centre. So it is definitely a major problem when these two different worlds, worlds that also are intertwined in all kinds of complicated ways, start to clash. Like you were saying earlier, Dharavi is the heart of the city and it sustains many basic needs of the city surrounding it.

JF: The recycling of hospital materials and other waste products, catering industries etc. all the out-sourcing happening in Dharavi.

JJ: Again, as we were saying about the risk of the romantic image we are starting to paint here, it is important to remember that a lot of these industries are hazardous; for those who live there, for the environment and these things are not desirable. This is why there is an industrial area in the SRA plans for example, and these are things that definitely have to be talked about.

JF: There is one final thing that I would like to mention about out-sourcing that relates to our project: when we were walking around looking at different printers, we came to a place off a narrow alley. It was basically a dimly lit room where a man sat with iron profiles stamping out cardboard boxes. These boxes had the logo of one of the largest banks in the world printed on them. He was producing the packaging for next year's Christmas presents for bank employees.

JHE: I think that is a good example because it shows that our original process actually led us down other routes that might open up toward a more interesting, dynamic and complex view on the relationships between the formal and the informal.

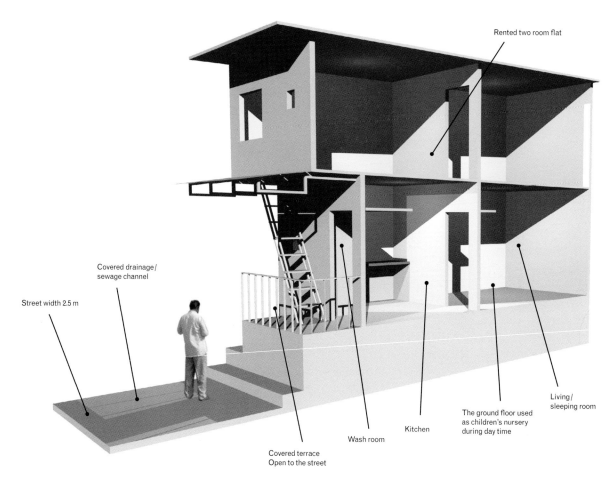

Rented two room flat

Covered drainage/
sewage channel

Street width 2.5 m

Wash room

Kitchen

The ground floor used
as children's nursery
during day time

Living/
sleeping room

Covered terrace
Open to the street

2:15

PV New Chawl

Buildings on PV New Chawl are a mix of live/work spaces, family homes, single use businesses and social/religious buildings. Buildings are one and two storey terraced buildings, sometimes built as single houses, sometimes in rows of up to five houses together.

House widths range from 1.6 to 4 metres. Depths of houses varied greatly reaching 8 metres, all houses being single sided with daylight from the street elevation. Houses

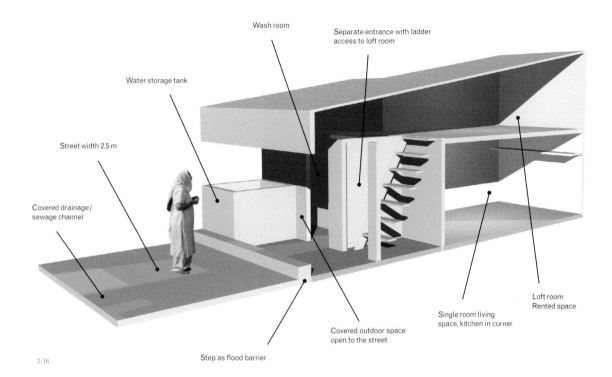

Wash room

Separate entrance with ladder
access to loft room

Water storage tank

Street width 2.5 m

Covered drainage/
sewage channel

Loft room
Rented space

Single room living
space, kitchen in corner

Covered outdoor space
open to the street

Step as flood barrier

2:16

— the Houses

often have partial walls on three sides with no private open
space behind the houses. Buildings generally have a semi-
public terrace facing onto the street, often one step up from
street level. These have a social function for the street as well
as for hanging washing, preparing food etc.

The houses that we studied have water stored in tanks
and an electricity supply. We measured two houses on PV
New Chawl, both were built by the owners.

Examples of typical two
storey houses, PV New
Chawl.

2:15   Meldridge's house.

2:16   Shakti Mari family's
house.

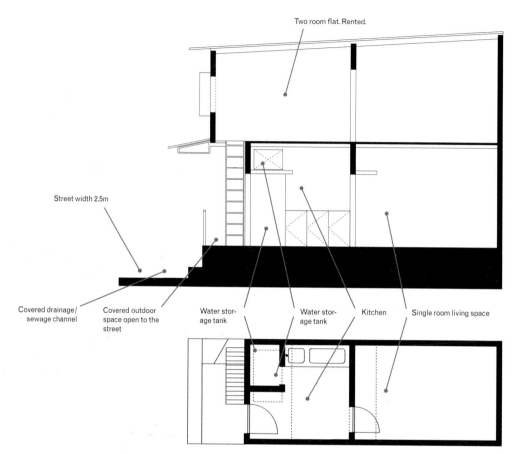

Two room flat. Rented.

Street width 2.5m

Covered drainage/
sewage channel

Covered outdoor
space open to the
street

Water stor-
age tank

Water stor-
age tank

Kitchen

Single room living space

2:17

2:19

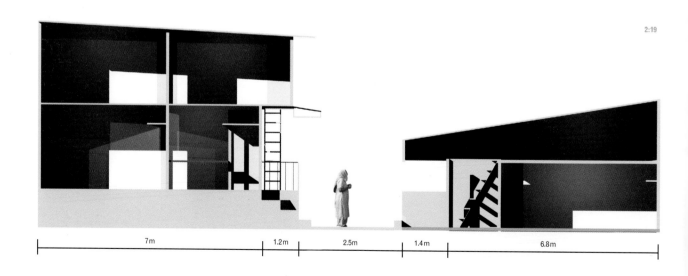

| 7m | 1.2m | 2.5m | 1.4m | 6.8m |

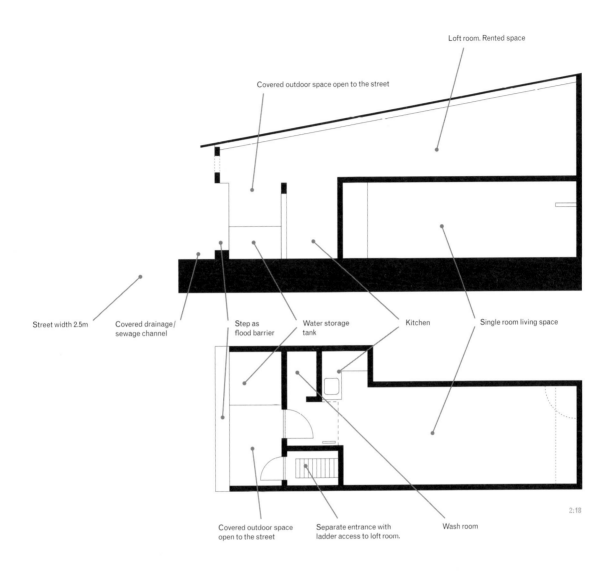

Loft room. Rented space

Covered outdoor space open to the street

Street width 2.5m

Covered drainage/
sewage channel

Step as
flood barrier

Water storage
tank

Kitchen

Single room living space

Covered outdoor space
open to the street

Separate entrance with
ladder access to loft room.

Wash room

2:18

2:17   Section and plan of
        Shakti Mari Family
        house.
        Scale 1:100

2:18   Section and plan of
        Meldridge's house.
        Scale 1:100

2:19   Typical section of street,
        PV New Chawl.
        Scale 1:200

2:20

A PORTABLE GRINDSTONE

A man has set up his grindstone on a reinforced bicycle frame and attached the driving belt.
Sitting on the baggage carrier, he pedals the grindstone at an even pace. The baggage carrier
is also reinforced with iron, forged in a spiral, and along with the solid stand this creates
stability. A small stock of knives, files and pliers are visible. The knife being sharpened is
made from used brand-iron steel. It belongs to the young Chinese proprietor dressed in a
black T-shirt. Soon he will take his sharpened knife and prepare the vegetables before he
lights up the gas beneath his wok. He makes food on the corner of Poonawalla and the street
called 60 Feet Road and places plastic chairs for his guests by the roadside in the afternoon.
The empty pink bucket in the foreground shows that the man carrying it has been to the
public toilets at the other end of Poonawalla. Every morning there is a march of men who
walk to the toilet buildings with buckets full of water to flush and return with empty buckets.
The women go there earlier, preferably before dawn.   *SE*

2:21

2:22

2:21 The bakery is one of the largest buildings on the street.

2:22 Community Centre, Poona–walla

2:23 The Pillai family have a single-storey house with a loft. They are Tamil people, as are many others on this street. On the far left, Chandana – their neighbour. From left to right: Shalini, Sita, Nilami, Akansha and Laxmé.

2:23

Poonawalla By Night

2:24 Waiting for customers. In this shop all necessities are found like in any supermarket. In the hot season, night time is the time to move around and do the shopping.

2:25 Despite the lack of public infrastructure, Poonawalla is lit by the inhabitants themselves as a collective effort to make life a little more comfortable.

2:25

2.26

2:27

2:26   Meldridge has a school-class at 8 pm. The children are answering the questions in chorus and their voices are heard over Poonawalla.

2:27   The market place stays open long after sunset – until the costumers go to bed. Everything from fresh vegetables to party-balloons can be bought here.

2:28   Night sky over Poonawalla. On a later visit we learn that Poonawalla is named after the original owner, Mr. Poona. Today ownership issues are more complex. Many people still pay rent for their housing.

CHAPTER 3

DENSITY AND INFRASTRUCTURE

Measuring Growth

Mumbai has grown fast. From 4 to 13 million inhabitants in 40 years, similarly Dharavi's estimated increase from approximately 102,000 original inhabitants in the sixties to today's estimates of between 376,000 and over 600,000. The reason for this variation is that neither the original census nor contemporary ones are entirely reliable. To ask how many people live at a certain address is a tricky question, and the answer depends on who is asking and who is answering. A house owner might say how many family members there are, but not how many he is subletting to. Those who live at work might not regard this as there home address even if they live there most of the year. Others might not want to give an address at all if they are suspicious of institutions and others fear taxation or eviction if they say how many people are living under the same roof.

In some cases it might be preferable to say how many there are in a household. It might be a question of formal rights, taking part in a rehabilitation programme offered by the city or some form of economic gain. However, this seems to be less common than a mistrust of official representatives of formal society's structures.

The official number of inhabitants is 376,000. This figure is the basis for the calculations on density and other statistics by the Kamla Raheja Vidyanidhi Institute for Architecture. The local NGO The Society for the Promotion of Area Resource Centres (SPARC), have made a survey which comes to 500,000 – 600,000. Even if one is sceptical about which figures to believe, it is clear that Dharavi's informal expansion is developing faster than it can be quantified. *JHE / ML*

Politics of Defecation

The water and sanitation systems are the veins of a city, and this system needs a strong heart of well functioning and regular maintenance. The heart could perhaps be a metaphor for Human Rights. In the often invisible water and sanitation system the values of a society are revealed. Water and sanitation is a matter that involves questions of democracy, gender, class and human rights. When water is provided to the poor people's homes, girls can go school, relieved from their daily duty of fetching water. When a neighbourhood is provided with sanitation, the mortality rates among children decrease, and when water and sanitation service is available to everyone a truly democratic society can be built. Looking at the amount of people covered by the water and sanitation system in India, one can bluntly state that there is a lot more to be done in "the largest democracy in the world".

Without water there can be no life. With only a little, dirty or contaminated water morbidity and mortality rates increase due to diarrhea and other water borne diseases. Living informally implies an insecure source of water, physical work or economical expenses in order to get hold of it. While the middle class tap water for next to nothing, the poor can end up paying five or six times the price due to profiteers. Corrupt officials surround the poorest charging the last coin for things that others might take for granted. The chain of bribery and corruption in the context of water and sanitation goes from the very bottom up to the very top in the society and is a political hotspot, especially now when resources are insecure due to irregularities in the climate and an increasing pressure on urban water services. And the poor suffer the most and pay the highest prices for water – financially, socially and physically.

In a country like Sweden the daily consumption of fresh drinking water per person is 180–200 litres. In informal areas without the formal water service, one person needs at the least ten litres of water a day for drinking, cooking and washing, to avoid the risk of illness caused by contaminated water. Children and the already weak are the most vulnerable. The major diseases are diarrhoea, cholera, dysentery, salmonella along with ascaris, giardia and other pathogen organisms and parasites. These diseases are easily treated when medical care is available. However, these diseases are the most common cause of death among the poor more than half of the people in the developing countries carry one or more of them.

Distressed, malnourished or ill adults are very vulnerable to water related diseases, radically reducing the prospects of upholding a livelihood.

Water and hygiene stands in a fragile dependency to each other. Access to running water is a condition for a satisfying level of hygiene that, apart from holding disease back, in turn keeps water clean. In congested informal areas it is hard to keep hygiene at a sufficient level. The storage of household water can often be a source of illness. Insects that just have visited the latrine will contaminate the water, and due to a lack of options or knowledge, people will use the same water for washing as for cooking or drinking. In a settled chawl like Poonawalla, most households have a covered concrete water cistern that is refilled regularly, but in other less developed areas it is common to see open, former chemical drums serving as household water containers.

SANITATION

Sanitation has proven to be a women's concern, as it is a matter of dignity. Privacy, away from the gaze of others, is a priority. The distress that comes with a lack of privacy has many consequences. Girls might reject school if there are no toilets provided, if the level of hygiene is low or doors are missing. Women might be forced to use the unsecure night hours to get out of sight. Most middle class experiences of defecating in public, stretches as far as letting the water run in a public toilet, to hide the plopping sound, and using vast amounts of soap to cover the odour, before sneaking out with a slight feeling of shame. In Dharavi at one point there were about two thousand people to one public toilet. A quick calculus would mean that one would have to stand in line for seven days before getting five minutes of toilet time. Of course people had to use the open space or so called "flying toilets" (plastic bags, thrown away).

When the National Slum Dwellers Federation implemented their toilet building scheme, the situation improved tremendously; from two thousand to fifteen per toilet. One of the greatest improvements was the children's department, with smaller holes and a rod to hold on to. Previously, children had fallen in to the holes sized for adults, a traumatic if not lethal experience. Still many children have to defecate in the open, as the children's toilets demand a fee of one rupee. This is not insignificant: a woman with three children who makes 30 rupees a day would have to pay at least fifteen percent of the wage for all visits needed in a day. However, the building of toilets shows immediate results. Less defecation in the open reduces contaminated water, lowering the illnesses and mortality rates.

According to the World Health Organization's analysis of the economical benefits of the provision of sustainable water and sanitation services – every invested dollar has $3–34

3:2

3:2   As time passes, the
      ground between the two
      pipelines will become
      more and more hidden
      beneath the litter. The
      area may even fill up
      and compact so much
      that the garbage will
      eventually become solid
      enough to be built on,
      just like parts of the Old
      Town in central Stock-
      holm, Sweden.

3:3   Women washing their
      clothes outside their
      houses built on the
      pipelines, under Mahim
      Sion Liak road.

economic return. This is due to the reduction in healthcare costs and the gained working days when adults are less ill. The Millennium Development Target No 10 is to half
the population without sustainable access to drinking water and basic sanitation by 2015.
Simultaneously, urban growth is so fast that the demands on existing water and sanitation
systems are far beyond capacity. In a mega city like Mumbai the situation is becoming very
fragile. The city is now facing a severe water shortage, due to the water consuming residents
and industries failing to recycle water, and the continual pollution of the rivers.

For a great deal of the middle class, the access to clean water, sanitation and effective
healthcare, implies security against water borne epidemics or shortage. It might then be
hard to see water and sanitation as a mutual societal problem, as long as there is no direct
threat of epidemics or protests from the poor. This lack of insight and responsibility is easily
interpreted as indifference. Water is politics, and the middle class are of political importance
for the government as their voters. The poor are not. According to governmental numbers
12 million out of almost 19 million citizens are provided with basic water and sanitation. By
leaving the rest of the population out of the services the government unconsciously sends
out a signal to the poor, easily understood as – you are not a fully fledge citizen. Then the
city is not only facing a shortage of water, but also a shortage in the important trust in the
democratic society.

AE

3:3

3:4

3:5

3:4   Drinking water is precious and is collected in all sorts of containers depending on whether it is found or bought.

3:5   Formal water pipes and a waste water canal. To get the water from the tank-cars or from the public pipes where it can sometimes be taken, there is a fabric of pipes running through the neighbourhood. During the rainy season open ditches end up in the channel which eventually empties the waste into Mahim Creek and further on into the Indian ocean.

3:6   (Pages 118–119.) Two pipelines transport the drinking water to Mumbai from Nothern Maharastra. These pipes are an example of the official infrastucture that serve people who have legal righs and citizenship in the city. The pipelines run into Mumbai over the marshlands surrounding Dharavi to the North and then through Dharavi. Here, they serve as walkways and workplaces. Sometimes people drill holes through the pipe to collect the water, which of course is strictly forbidden.

3:6

Dharavi in Figures

According to figures presented at the Urban Age India Conference in November 2007, formally 17.8 million people live in the Mumbai Metropolitan Region and the average population density of Greater Mumbai's 438 square kilometres is 27,348 persons per square kilometre. The density of Dharavi is about 10 times this – around 250,000 persons per square kilometre. 61% of the population growth is due to natural increase [births as opposed to migration]. 81% of jobs are in the service sector.

Mumbai is a pedestrian city. There are 344,817 registered cars. 2% of all trips are made in private cars and 55% by walking. There has been a 420% increase in auto rickshaws over the last 15 years making traffic a growing problem. However, traffic is not a big problem inside Dharavi where almost all journeys are taken by foot, on charts, bicycles or motorbikes.On average, 19 people are killed every day in traffic related accidents.

6.5 million people make use of the 300 kilometre long suburban rail system each day. Two of these lines surround Dharavi and connect it with the rest of the city. On these crowded trains women prepare dinner, commuters take a nap and some people even manufacture simple products.

43% of Greater Mumbai is green space, 48% of all slums are built on private land and an estimated 56% of households lack toilets.

10 million people in the Mumbai Metropolitan region live in slums.

COMPOSITION OF NAGARS

Dharavi is composed of over 85 Nagars, which in turn are further sub-divided into many housing societies, chawl societies etc. A Nagar originally meant a town – eg Ahmednagar. But in the Dharavi context, it is a description for a geographical area which its residents feel they belong to. It need not be recognized by postal or municipal authorities.

The term Chawl initially refers to a so called "ground + 2 or 3-floor structure" initially built by the British for migrant workers and their families. They had a common corridor and common toilets and an area of around 14 – 16 square metres, but in the Dharavi context it is used more generally.   *JHE/AE*

3:7   The composition of
Nagars in Dharavi.   Source: Urban Age India Conference, November 2007.

3:8

3:9

3:10

LANDUSE IN DHARAVI

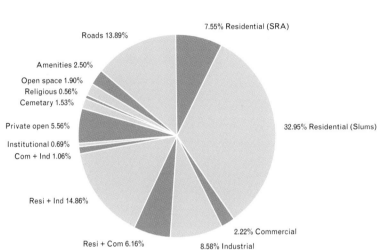

Roads 13.89%
Amenities 2.50%
Open space 1.90%
Religious 0.56%
Cemetary 1.53%
Private open 5.56%
Institutional 0.69%
Com + Ind 1.06%
Resi + Ind 14.86%
Resi + Com 6.16%
7.55% Residential (SRA)
32.95% Residential (Slums)
2.22% Commercial
8.58% Industrial

LANDUSE IN MUMBAI

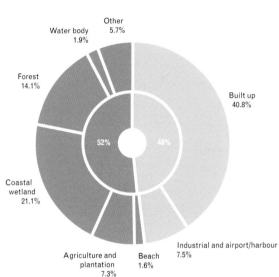

Other 5.7%
Water body 1.9%
Forest 14.1%
Coastal wetland 21.1%
Agriculture and plantation 7.3%
Beach 1.6%
Industrial and airport/harbour 7.5%
Built up 40.8%
52%   48%

MUMBAI'S SLUM LANDOWNERSHIP

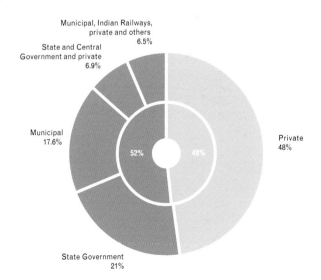

Municipal, Indian Railways, private and others 6.5%
State and Central Government and private 6.9%
Municipal 17.6%
State Government 21%
Private 48%
52%   48%

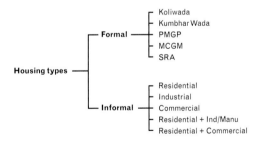

Housing types
Formal
- Koliwada
- Kumbhar Wada
- PMGP
- MCGM
- SRA

Informal
- Residential
- Industrial
- Commercial
- Residential + Ind/Manu
- Residential + Commercial

3:8
Area of marshland
along the Mithi River
and Mahim Creek.

3:9
Flooding / Choking
zones in Dharavi.

3:10
Hospitals (yellow)
Schools (red)
Open spaces (green)

Source of information: Kamla Raheja Vidyanhidi Institute for Architecture, 2006/07

The Private Doctor's Office

The paediatrician's office is situated in a block of flats on the outskirts of Dharavi. On the second floor of the dark stairwell there is an insignificant door that leads into the waiting room. It is eleven o'clock and the office has just opened. The small waiting room with simple wooden benches is almost empty except for two mothers and their children. The posters on the wall warn against hepatitis, HIB diseases (meningitis, pneumonia, blood-poisoning, etc.) and encourage child vaccination. A nurse takes notes concerning the patients. The waiting room starts to fill up with mothers and their children, entire families, and a few men with their children. As the room becomes full, the men step out into the stairwell. The doctor has not arrived yet.

Like many other doctors, this paediatrician moves between different clinics. She works in a hospital close to Dharavi, at this private office where she receives children from Dharavi for a low fee and finally at her own office for middle and upper class children, which is her main source of income.

When she invites us in to her room we notice there is barely enough space for everything. The place is filled with an examination table placed on top of a cabinet, a small scale for weighing the children, toys to distract reluctant patients, instruments, a table and some chairs.

She tells us that the worst diseases are airborne, like TBC, since these diseases spread easily in the poor air circulation where families share a few cubic metres. During the rainy season cholera and diarrhoea increase dramatically due to poor water quality. A general problem is the difficulties of personal care, because of the scarcity of bathrooms, together with the struggle to keep cooking hygienic.

JW

3:11

3:12

3:11 Outside the office, a family is on their way to pay a visit to the doctor.

3:12 The desk barely fits into the small space.

3:13 The examination table has been placed on top of a cabinet. There is a small scale and a few toys in the window.

3:13

Congested Space

The most congested parts of Dharavi are where the problems are congested too. No daylight, the constant risk of fire and problems with rats and bugs. Air- and waterborne diseases can flourish here, especially during monsoon season when the area can be under water. Ditches flood and sewage water pours into the houses. The families all have to cramp up together and sleep on lofts and build up other arrangements when the floor is under water.

However, one of the most difficult things in daily life here is being a woman. For instance, in order to find her way to a public toilet, a woman needs to walk through the narrow maze of walkways and faces the risk of being harassed or offended. it is impossible to keep a proper distance to anyone you meet on your way here no matter whether it is day time or night time.

ML

3:14 This narrow alley is in fact a
covered sewage ditch. Two
major problems dominate
this crowded living situation:
first of all, the ditches flood
during the monsoon season
and sewage water pours into
the houses. Secondly, the air
does not circulate properly in
the houses when the alleys
are so narrow and ventilation
is almost non-existent. This
congested environment is a
serious fire hazard and the
enclosed spaces are a risk
for the spread of airborne
diseases.

3:15   The poorest people live in the most congested parts of Dharavi. They do not have enough space nor can they afford bricked water-cisterns. They must make do with plastic barrels. These blue barrels come to Dharavi full of chemicals for use in various trades, such as the leather industry. When they have served their original purpose, the barrels are washed and sold as water containers.

3:16   The alley is narrow but it offers cool and shade. The activities in the small area between the houses can vary during the course of the day. They can become a workplace, a kitchen, a laundry or place to do homework. In this image the space is being used for the manufacture of flower garlands, which will be sold and later offered to the temple.

3:17   Some alleys even lack the loose stones or cement slabs that normally cover a sewage ditch. In the water bacteria, micro-organisms and larva thrive. At night the open ditches are used as toilets.

3:18   Congestion and social oppression characterises life in these areas of high
density. Daylight barely reaches down into the alley and during certain hours the
cooking vapours lie like a mist in these shaft-like environments.

3:19 Even the densest of structures offer meeting places, like here in a crossing between three different alleys. The lack of infrastructure encourages people to take their own initiatives. Electricity, sewage and rain gutters are arranged collectively using the materials at hand.

3:20   3:20

Public Infrastructure — Details

In every part of Dharavi people care about their quality of life as much as they can. Even though there is a lack of public spaces, communal places exists on a small scale. Places to rest and meet appear in corners and in the streets, street lights are scarce but light up, here and there. Signs are painted onto walls and decorations appear spontaneously.

Whilst looking at the structure of Dharavi and PV New Chawl we also recorded the small details: the street, the furnishings and the utilities. There is a long list of standard components to a street that are often overlooked by the user, from lighting, post boxes, seating, signage, rainwater drainage, traffic barriers etc. PV New Chawl and the surrounding streets and squares of Dharavi also contain many of the same services found in formal city streets, however, here they are mostly ad-hoc, handmade solutions.

JHE / JF

3:21   3:21

3:22

3:22

3:22

3:22

3:20 Many of the connective
      infrastructure, which are
      usually hidden underground
      in formal streets can be seen
      here on the surface, the wires,
      pipes and cables showing the
      network of utilities required for
      a street to work.

3:21 Bespoke street signage.

3:22 As well as the appropriation
      of found objects to provide
      the basic infrastructure, one
      can also see more decorative
      or social solutions, including
      plants, seating and even
      playground equipment.

3:23 A salvaged municipal bench.

3:23

3:24

3:24

3:24 Street lighting is provided from innumerable sources, mostly from house frontages.

3:25 Electricity is taken from local boxes. Electricity is also taken from a pole on the outskirts of Dharavi and the electricity company simply pay semi-formal visits to collect payments. Ironically this system often means that the poor end up paying more than the middle class for their electricity.

3:26 A home made slide typically placed on a corner of a public street.

3:27 Among the improvised solutions for infrastructure like electrical power and sewage one can also find beautiful, meticulous details: a painted door, an image on a wall or a plastic flower by the window.

3:28 Internet access and a number of pay phones are available on PV New Chawl.

3:29 Steel pipes used to control traffic in a pedestrian street.

3:30 A barber's hand-painted sign.

3:25

3:26

3:20

3:24

3:27

3:28

3:28

3:29

3:30

3:31   Occasionally the structure opens up, like in this area, close to the railway.
Here, the stairs serve as public seating in the shade.

Vicinities

3:32

It seems to me that many women are restricted to a daily environment that does not stretch far beyond home.

The Kadam family's daughters rarely leave their local neighbourhood in Dharavi. One day I told them I had been to the Kanchan Beauty Parlour on Balaji Nagar with Preema. They thought that this was very far away. They had never been there themselves, a walk of no more than 45 minutes for them. It seems that women and girls may not or dare not move freely. Since girls do not seem to play much outdoors when they are small, their territory becomes very limited from an early age.

In a stationary environment like this entrepreneurs do not need to rent business facilities, which also suits an informal economy. Business is conducted on the street and sellers carry most of their goods along with them.

The fishmonger marches along yelling, "Fresh fish! Fresh fish!" as another man comes down the street with a basket balancing on his head adding his call of, "Fresh fruit! Fresh fruit!" The ice-cream man has a slender cart that can be manoeuvred through narrow alleys. The cart's merry ringing is recognised by everyone. A honey seller walks along balancing a stainless steel can on his head. The grinder sets up his bicycle and connects the chain to a pedal-powered grindstone. Sitting on the bicycle saddle he sharpens knives and scissors. A bucket seller comes by, carrying a mountain of pink, yellow and green plastic buckets and bowls. The greengrocer stops pushing his heavy, unwieldy cart in order to weight up a couple of chilli peppers. He receives a coin and strenuously pushes on. They all seem inexhaustible.

This drawing shows a textile seller who has stopped by a wall, untied a white piece of protective cloth and is presenting all of his brightly coloured textiles for two women.

SE

3:32

"One cannot make any connection between mass housing and the work of two leading Indian architects, Charles Correa and Balkrishna Doshi. Both have in fact been active in the field of housing, designing low-rise, high-density schemes for the middle classes (all planned housing in India is intended for the middle classes)."

CAREL WEEBER,
THE INDIAN ANGEL

3:34

BEHIND MAHIM STATION

One of the most dense areas of Dharavi lies behind Mahim Station. The street can be described as a kind of square tunnel where the ground is made up of slabs of concrete which have been laid over piping and a hand-dug sewer ditch. The houses are also built on this concrete, which is under street level. The sun hardly reaches down here even in the middle of the day, and the concrete stays relatively cool. Perfect for bare feet to tread upon.   *SE*

3:33

3:33   The alley is so narrow that a man can sit on the rooftop with his legs dangling over the edge and easily repair the house on the other side of the alley.

3:34   The Das family, two adults and two children, live in a contested area right behind Mahim Station. They originally came from Calcutta in Bengal.

3:35

3:35

CRICKET

Open spaces in Dharavi account for only two percent of the total area. These areas are known as multi-use spaces.

In the leather district there is an open space where hides are set out to dry after the tanning process. When this area is not being used it becomes a temporary cricket ground.

ML

3:35 A cricket match in
a multi-use space.
A board from the
construction site nearby
serves as a bat.

3:36 Note the writing on the
wall: "Bombay Boys
Cricket Club". A woman
is drying hides, while a
young boy is improving
his swing with the bat.

CHAPTER 4

PRODUCTION

Made In Dharavi

Dharavi is not only a place to dwell, the site is also a huge employer. It is said that the number of people who come to Dharavi everyday for work is greater than those leaving it for jobs in the city.

The values of the businesses here have been estimated at millions of Euro but no one can know for sure. A large part of the production never enters the books of an accountant and it is difficult to get an overview even from inside the area.

Workshops of all kinds, recycling, plastic industry, food, printing and leather are big businesses. But you can find highly qualified craftsmen in almost any field such as potters, tailors and carpenters along with food and catering services that serve the entire Mumbai area.

A lot of products are made for the international market, commonly components will be produced from recycled material before it is being shipped off and assembled elsewhere. We found the most banal everyday objects being produced on a large scale with recycled plastic in Dharavi: plastic tags that are used as underwear holders in European stores, suitcase wheels and paper files. Leather for a vast variety of purposes as well as many different kinds of paper products. But we also found very high-tech products. One example is the surgical thread produced from the intestines of goats at the Johnson & Johnson factory.

There is also a local economy of salesmen and various services, from beauty parlours to fishmongers. Sometimes the local and the international markets coincide, as in the case of recycled syringes that serve as candy cases.

A lot of the production is run from the home. Families will engage in common investments and many producers co-operate with neighbouring workshops, perhaps sitting on the floor cutting off thread ends from a nearby jeans factory.

One can assume that every household in the North owns something made in Dharavi.

THE RECYCLING INDUSTRY

SORTING THE GARBAGE

When the garbage arrives to Dharavi it is dumped off the bridge in big bags or containers. Already when collected in the city, the garbage has gone through some rough sorting: metal, glass and plastics have been separated. At night you can see the garbage pickers all over the city sorting the household waste. Now the work of careful sorting begins. Different kinds of plastics goes to different recycling workshops to be ground and melted. Some things like containers can be used and sold again as second hand products after being cleaned.

PLASTIC

In the noisy plastic workshop, the air is filled with dust. All kinds of plastic are being cleaned and separated into smaller pieces. When the plastic has been chopped up, the flakes are dried in the sun before being packed into big bags.

WATER BOTTLE RECYCLING

4.2   Garbage is stored in big bags on the rooftops. In the middle of the recycling district there is a large mosque under construction.

4.3   Children learn early the value of waste.

4:4   The step between garbage and resource is only a matter of sorting.

Water bottles are collected all over Mumbai for recycling here in Dharavi. The paper wrap is torn off by hand and recycled as well.

When the bottles have been stripped of their paper and blue cap, the bottles are taken to small workshops around the area. The plastic is chopped into small flakes that can either be exported or melted into pellets for further use in the plastic industry. China is a big buyer of this kind of crude plastic. New products are made for further export around the globe.

A lot of the things we use to sit on, like cushions, soft seats as well as blankets have a kind of stuffing made from these recycled bottles. Also the popular material for clothing called fleece originates from these bottles.   *ML*

4:2

4:3

4:4

4:5

4:5 Industrial buildings in the recycling district are sometimes monuments of recycled material in themselves. The architecture of sheet-metal glows at sunset.

4.6 The poor people in India take care of the blue chemical barrels when they are emptied and cleaned. They are re-used as containers for drinking water.

4:7 Bags filled with bottles, soon to become something else.

4:6

4:8

4.8 Fresh grapes and re-
cycled buckets for sale.

4:9 Clear plastic pellets
being dyed pink. These
pellets are sold as fresh,
new raw material. It is
used both in Dharavi
and sold for export.

4:10 Women and young men
stripping labels off
water bottles.

4:9

4:10

4:11 Some of the garbage comes from a hospital nearby. After cleaning, they are taken apart. Some of the parts are melted and recycled into new plastic. But the outer parts of the syringe are re-used at once. When they have been plugged, they become containers for a special kind of sweet powder sold as candy.

4.12 Interior in a plastic workshop.

4.13 Sorting syringes.

4:12

4:13

LEATHER PRODUCTION

TANNING

Tanning is the process that
occurs after the skin is stripped from an animal, when
all fur, blood and fat is taken
off the hide. There are two
different ways of tanning
hides: chemical tanning with
chromium sulphur, or the
vegetable process. Chro-
mium tanning is the most
common method and today
more than 90% of the world's
hides are tanned chemically.
Chromium Sulphur causes
acute toxicity to water dwelling organisms and if it leaks
into lakes or rivers it will kill
many fish.

As well as the potters from Gujarat, leather production was one of the first industries to
establish itself in Dharavi. All forms of slaughter, skin and leather treatment are made by
the caste-less or non-Hindu groups. The Muslim tanners in Dharavi migrated from the
Tamil Nadu to Mumbai (Bombay) in the mid 1800s. They settled in what at the time was
the outskirts of Mumbai. The city soon grew around them and they had to move out parts
of their production that were regarded as unclean and not appropriate for a city centre.

The tanners moved north to the swampy outskirts of Mumbai and the first tannery was
settled in Dharavi 1887. The production grew steadily as migrating workers moved into
Mumbai, searching for work.

Tanning is undoubtedly a hazardous job. It is unhealthy for the workers and the environment, and appropriate precautions must be taken. The situation in Dharavi, with its lack
of infrastructure means that even the most rudimentary laws concerning pollution or the
health of workers cannot be followed.

For anyone living in or around Dharavi, the chemical problems must have been less
important than the stench from the tanneries. The hides and the waste products from the
tanning process would quickly start to spread strong odour and be a source of infectious
disease in the high temperature. Tanning demands a very high level of hygiene and cleaning
in order to be odourless and in a poor area without a functioning sewage system or clean
water it is impossible to keep the level of hygiene needed.

PAST, PRESENT

Because the tanning industry cannot follow industrial or environmental regulations, production becomes an environmental threat. The contamination of Mahim River started at
the beginning of the land filling in the early 1800s. The rapidly expanding chemical tanning
industry in Dharavi caused toxic emissions which finally killed all the fish in the river, leaving the Koli fishermen without their traditional means of income.

In the 1980s the authorities banned every kind of tanning within Dharavi or central
Mumbai, directing production to Deonar, north of the Mumbai region. The leather industries now buys tanned hides from Deonar where approximately 40,000 goats (year 2000)
are slaughtered every week. Some unofficial tanning activity is surely taking place closer
to Dharavi than to Deonar. The leather industry is globally expanding as the demand for
leather is increasing. In China for example, the expansion of the leather industry is causing
conflicts with the fishing industry.

INTO THE SKIN

Tanning is the second step in the chain of leather goods production, after the preparatory stages. The third process is called crusting. In short, this is when the hide is thinned out, re-tanned and oiled. The culmination of this process is the drying, softening and dyeing operations.

When wet after the tanning, the hides are dried, often in the sun on rooftops. This makes the hides as stiff as cardboard. The next step is therefore to soften them with wooden rollers, which is a very dusty job. After the softening process, the hides are dyed.

The first step of the dyeing process involves large rotating wooden barrels, where the entire hide is dyed. A second surface coating or finishing is then added. Commonly paint is sprayed onto the leather surface. The chemical base of the colours used for finishing often contains isocyanates.

As a comparison to the tanning process in Dharavi we might look at Sweden where industrial exposure to isocyanates is rigorously regulated. Here, wearing a full face mask and having medical check ups every six months are mandatory. In Dharavi you can hardly find any facilities for workers protection. Most of the final spraying is done outdoors for the fresh air, but in a congested area like Dharavi, these streets are often very close to residential units.

If the tanning before 1980 created a widely spread stench of putrefaction in Dharavi – it is the intensively penetrating smell of hazardous chemicals that prevails today.

ENTREPRENEURS

Some parts of the processed hides are sold to the national and international market, and others stay in Dharavi, where a whole production chain of leather goods can be found. It is an impressive variation of goods and qualities. Most of the leather manufacturers in Dharavi are formally registered companies, making business on the global market, but even though the company is formal, the production might not be. Many of the workers are not covered by any laws or legislation and many of them are underpaid. Certain parts of the production will often be subcontracted to others to do certain parts of the manufacturing, such as sewing, applique or braiding. This chain of production could easily be mistaken as a succession of entrepreneurs. But the further away from the registered company the production lies, the more informal and unsecured the conditions are for the workers. A lot of this work is executed by underpaid women in their homes.

Dharavi is well known for its leather production in Mumbai and along Sion Bandra Linkroad there are all kinds of exclusive goods for sale in various shops. Customers come from all over the city. Here you find everything from Prada bags to everyday sandals. The goods produced in Dharavi are included in an extensive global market, where the origin of the product is erased on its way to the consumer.

Made in India.

AE

ISOCYANATES

Isocyanates are compounds containing the isocyanates group (-NCO). They react with compounds containing alcohol (hydroxyl) groups and produce polyurethane paint and other polyurethane based products. Jobs that may involve exposure to isocyanates include painting, shoemaking and use of adhesives. Isocyanates also include compounds like carcinogen, which can cause cancer. The main effects of long term exposure are allergy, asthma and other lung problems, irritated skin and muscular membranes.

4:14   The workers outside the leather factory.

4:15   A goat skin, dyed and ready for the final drying.

4:16   Samples of various colours and qualities.

4:17   Sandals and shoes being assembled in a cramped room with poor ventilation. The vapours from the glue make the air very heavy. The shoes will be exported to Germany.

4:18   An extremely dusty process of thinning the hides. The workers have to find their own protective clothing.

4:14

4:15

4:16

4:17

4:18

4:19

THE PRINTING INDUSTRY

4:19   Chamunda paper and
       board suppliers.

4:20   A small offset printers.

4:21   Business cards from
       a number of printers
       visited.

4:22   Die cutting for stickers
       and labels.

4:23   Examples of printing
       techniques in Dharavi.

Every part of the printing industry can be found in Dharavi – graphic designers, art directors, editors and printers. They have national and international customers. There is also a great variety of printing techniques, from peddle-driven letterpress machines, antique German offset printing presses, screen printing studios, to the latest digital printers. The printing industry we saw here ranges in scale from individuals based in homes or small premises, producing material for use within Dharavi, to large companies producing digitally printed Bollywood posters and roadside advertisements that can be up to 20 metres wide. Other associated businesses such as paper suppliers and die cutters can also be found.   *JF*

4:20

4:21

J/2, P. V. New Chawl, Opp. Abhyudaya Co op. Bank, Mahim(E), Mumbai-400017.

Tel.: 2403 1592 • Mobile: 98212 05336

Specialised in
Four colour designing & Printing
High Resolution Scanning

Modern Arts

Mani

S. Rajendran

COPIAM ARTS

ALL TYPE OF PRINTING WORKS

Shop B-42/2, Balaji Nagar, 90 Ft. Road, Opp. Police Stn.,
Dharavi, Mumbai - 400 017. Tel. : 2403 1591 • Fax : 2402 0399

Maharaj

Tel 2402 5716
2402 1409
2403 1879
2401 9006
Mobile 3510 4782

Chamunda Trading Co.

PAPER & BOARD WHOLESALER & RETAILERS

Shop N0. A/3, Opp. Venus Hotel, Near Police Station.
90 Feet Road, Dharavi, Mumbai - 400 017
E-mail. chamundatrading co@usa.net.com

4:22

4:23

4:24

4:25

POTTERIES

The potteries have a special place in this community, their businesses are as old as Dharavi itself. The clay comes from pits in the area. The houses here have an interesting design, they are long and have two entrances: one goes to the yard where production takes place and the other entrance faces the street where the goods are displayed and sold.

Not only has the pottery its own history, so have the houses and the outdoor spaces in the area. Every family has a house with two functions: a workshop and a home. In one end the craft, in the other the family. In the part where the pottery is created, there is a common yard where the goods can be finished and fired together with the neighbours' pots, cups, bowls, plates, and urns.   *SE*

4:27

4:26

4:25 A young girl watches us from the window.

4:26 Throwing a pot on a wooden wheel. The cups in the background are used once and then thrown away.

4:27 The various stages of the pots can be seen here. From the wet clay on the left to the polished end product on the right.

SURGICAL THREAD

Goat intestines are one of the products that have great value in both Dharavi and the rest of the world. Here, the art of making surgical thread has developed. The company Johnson & Johnson has a small factory on the outskirts of Dharavi for production and sterile packaging. The first steps in making this high quality product takes place in the vicinity of the leather area.

This laboratory is as clean as any lab, even if the interior may not look as high-tech as the hospital where it will be used. The care and knowledge invested here is exactly the same as in any medical establishment.

ML

4:28

4:28   Benches for preparing the intestines. The atmosphere is calm, the environment is neat and clean.

4:29   First, the intestines are soaked in order to rid any other remainder of the animal. Then, it is cleaned inside and out. The pride in this business is great – the surgical thread is supposed to be the best of its kind in the world.

4:31

4:32

4:30 In the leather district there are plenty of companies involved in the many steps of the business.

4:31 Intestines being soaked in water waiting for the next stage of refinement.

4:32 The Johnson & Johnson factory outside Dharavi is hidden behind walls.

4:33

TEXTILES

The textile industry is a big part of Dharavi's production. Entire products, but also out-sourced details pass through people's homes and workshops of various sizes. The textile production is aimed at the local as well as an international market.

JHE

4:33 Textile production is, a major business in Dharavi. The Dubai market craves cheap products. Here, five men are busy sewing jeans for the United Arab Emirate.

4:34 A lot of the textile production takes place in people's homes. It is mostly a woman's job to sew small sequins and pearls on to the garments or fabrics. These sets will be sold in Germany.

4:35   Bakery, snacks and other dry-foods are made all over Dharavi. in big scale and small.

4:36   Papadams are dried in the sun.

4:37   Dabas, or lunch boxes marked with colours and ready to be distributed.

4:38   A young man is stiring a pan full of chiki.

4:39   The two open fire stoves make the unventilated room very warm.

4:35

4:36

FOOD

THE DABBA MAKERS – AN ENTIRELY INFORMAL INDUSTRY

The world's most complex lunchtime food distribution network operates in Mumbai: an elaborate choreography where more than 200,000 tin lunch boxes (dabbas) are collected from kitchens and delivered to office and retail workers all across the city.

The concept of the lunchbox courier (dabbawala) originated in the 1880s when India was under British rule. Many British people who came to the colony did not like the local food, so a service was set up to bring lunch to these people in their workplace straight from their home. Today it is possible to order a delivery with a text message from a cell phone.

Dabbawalas usually cycle around the city, collecting dabbas from homes or, more often, from dabba makers. The dabbawala then takes the food packages to a designated sorting area, where they are sorted into groups. These groups of boxes are then marked with their destinations and mostly put on train coaches. These markings indicate which train station the boxes should be unloaded at as well the delivery address.

At each station the boxes are handed over to a local dabbawala, who delivers them. After lunch the empty boxes are collected and sent back to their respective kitchens or homes.

Over 200,000 lunch boxes are distributed every day by around 5,000 dabbawalas, who work for a nominal fee, but deliver with the utmost care and punctuality. According to a recent survey, there is only one mistake in every 16,000,000 deliveries.

The photo to the right (4:37) shows two yellow bags full of lunch boxes from one of the dabba kitchens. On the street below is one of the dabba kitchens in Dharavi. Two bags full of lunch boxes are waiting for the dabbawala to transport them to the right place – to the right hungry customer. We can see the simple but very precise markings on the handles, with different colours for the different districts.   *SE*

4:37

4:38

4:39

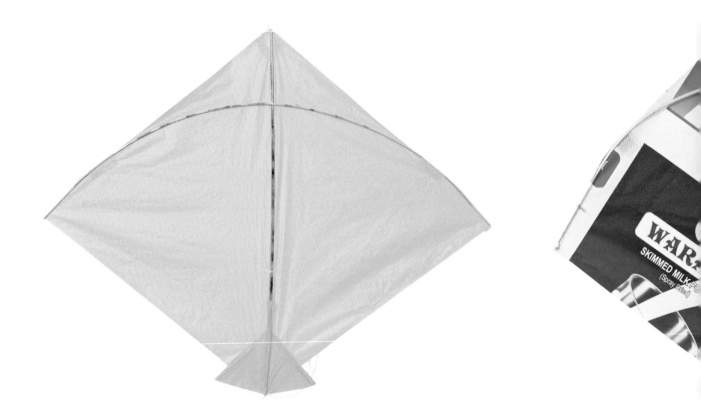

KITE FACTORY

Omar and Pablo work at the kite factory. "To make the kites we use recycled plastic, paper and cellophane from the Dharavi recycling business. The material used to be file folders, but the wood comes from Calcutta. The kites are not for export, they are made for the local market. We have worked here since we were small kids. We like to fly kites too."

"We usually fly a lot during January and February in Mumbai, and in December when we celebrate Diwali and Makar Sankranti. It is a great tradition.

"When we have kite fights it is just a game. We aim to cut off each other's strings by preparing our own kite strings with wheat flour and manja. Manja is a mix of ground glass and chemical glue. A kite costs 2 – 10 Rupees."   *LE*

4:40

4:40 Three different kites.
Silk paper and recycled
plastic are common
materials.

4:41 Omar and Pablo
Patangmart in the kite
factory.

4:41

4:41

CRAFTS AND SERVICE INDUSTRIES: SEVEN EXAMPLES

The size of Dharavi is a little more than 2 square kilometers. Within this structure, where more than 650 000 people live and work, there is not only trade and business aimed for both Indian and international markcts. There is also an extensive local businesslife, serving the community. Everything you can find in the formal city can be found here. Hairdressers, laundries, restaurants, cobblers, craftsmen, entertainers and grocery shops. You name it – and someone will take you to a specialized shop. Often it will be behind a small door, no bigger than hole in a wall or in somebody's home. But once you come inside you might be surprised to find a deeper knowledge and know-how than you would in the formal city.

ML

4:42   Vimal, the local photographer. Specific backgrounds are used for the wedding photo, the family portrait and other special occasions.

4:43   The construction of new buildings offer a lot of opportunities for construction work.

4:44   An electrician at work in an apartment in one of the newer buildings.

4:42

4:43

4:44

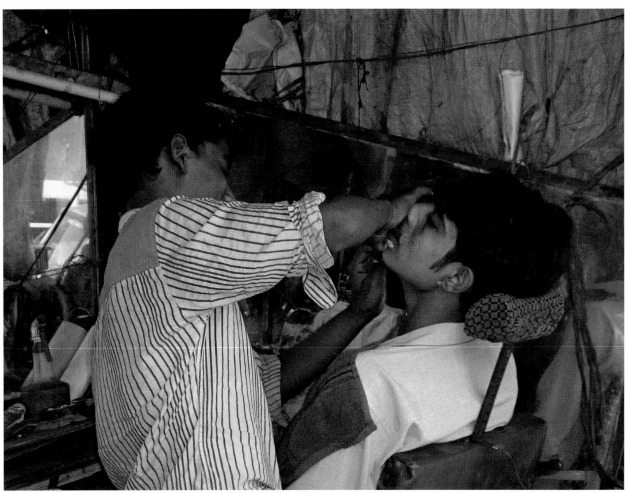

4:45

4:45 This barber shop is in the middle of a busy industrial area. There are many customers. Even if it might not look so comfortable, the results are pristine. This customer's newly shaved chin is as smooth as his earlobe.

4:46 With a large pestle and mortar this woman is making a delicious sticky mass which will be eaten together with deep-fried bread.

4:47 Old handicrafts are found all over Dharavi side by side with new inventions. The street is a place where all aspects of life coincide: social life, working for a living, cooking, washing, and play. Here, a woman is making brooms. Later, she will sell her goods in the street.

4:48 Making gates and fences for the middle class is a growing industry.

4:46

4:47

4:48

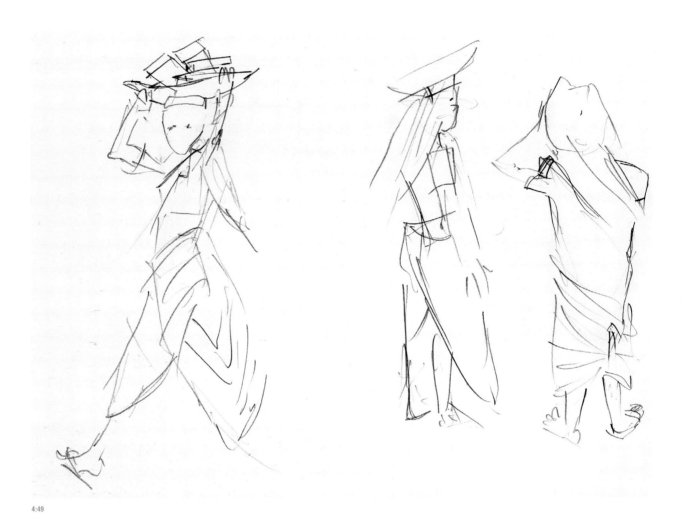

4:49

ROAD CONSTRUCTIONS

These women work with rebuilding a traffic island on the busy Dharavi-Sion Highway. The traffic island is supposed to be narrowed to create two lanes in either direction.

The women helped each other lift up the pails and buckets onto each other's heads. I wonder how much they weighed; they were filled to the rim with stones and bits of concrete torn out of the ground. From dusk until dawn the women hurried along in their slippery, plastic sandals to a place where they could dump their heavy loads. One can note their clothing and how they created a trouser-like piece of clothing by wrapping themselves in a colourful five-metre long cloth and pulling one end of it between their legs and tying it up at the waist. This allows them to move more freely in their strenuous chores.

As I am writing this, another scene comes to mind. At another construction site down-town, a woman is balancing a load on her head with one hand and holding her child with a steady grip in the other hand. The child, 2 – 3 years old, is walking barefoot in the gravel, tired and struggling to keep up. She could not afford the cost of a day nursery for her baby.   *SE*

4:50

4:51

4:50 This is an image of temporary living-quarters all lined up against a wall. Entire families follow various road constructions around, moving from place to place. The constructions consist of sheets of tarpaulin, cardboard and other scrap material. Here and there they have managed to pull out stones and anchor thin, wooden beams to stabilise the construction. I do not know what happens to these homes during the monsoon season.

4:51 The traffic-friendly result made it extremely difficult for pedestrians to cross. Dharavi is to the left and on the other side of the street, one of the rare public toilet buildings.

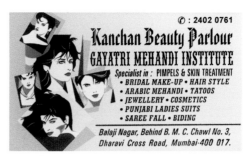

4:52   4:53

KANCHAN'S BEAUTY PARLOUR

4:52 The palm of a woman's
      hand has been deco-
      rated with mehendi.

4:53 Kanchan's visiting card.

4:54 Kanchan plucking
      eyebrows with a thread.
      She works very swiftly
      with a sharp and chic
      result. The customer will
      have a white line under
      her eyebrow for a few
      days until the sun tans
      her skin.

Kanchan is a Mumbai resident who has returned. She once lived in London for several years with her brothers. She studied there and speaks perfect English.

Kanchan tries to save as much as she can and her brother sends her money every month from London. Some of it goes to her mother and her siblings, and some of it to Kanchan's dream. She wants to buy her own house in Dharavi. She will continue to run her beauty parlour there.

Kanchan's Beauty parlour is popular. When I visited her there was a queue of customers lining up outside. "Why should I buy a house and open a salon in some other part of Mumbai?" she says. "I have all my customers here."

"I like it here in Dharavi. Close to work – it only takes a few minutes to walk here, and I feel safe in the area."

She estimates that she needs 6 lakh, which is 600,000 rupees. She is already on her way there and manages to save a couple of thousand each time Preema comes by from the credit and savings collective Mahila Milan.

Kanschan tells Preema that it will probably take another two years to save the whole amount. Preema responds by wagging her head in that particularly Indian manner which means "yes".

SE

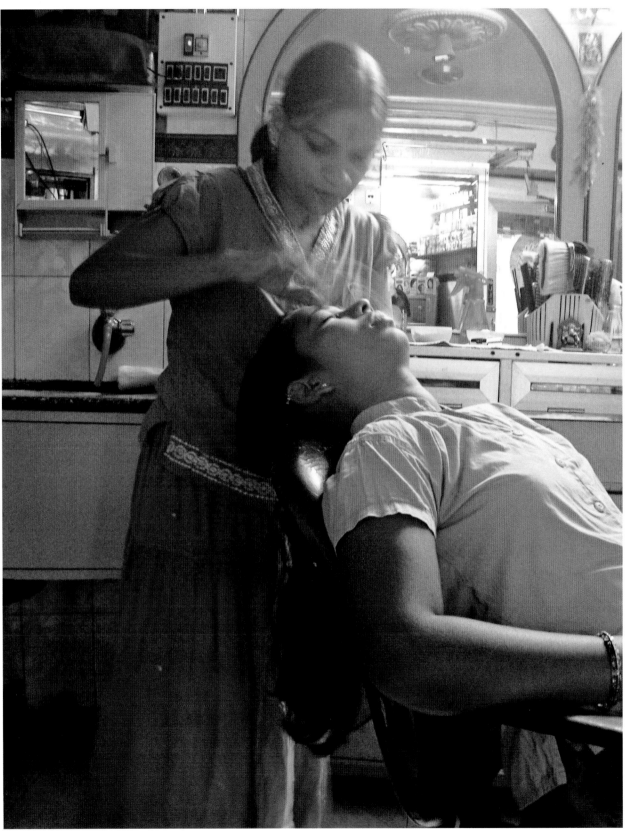

4:54

BUSINESSMEN

4:55

Dharavi is said to have a yearly turnover of more than ten billion Euro (if we choose to quote media sources like the Economist and the BBC). However, ten billion Euro could be too much or too little. As with everything else in the informal sector, figures are unreliable – especially when it comes to economy.

What we do know is that some people have become very rich through business in the area. Others have lost their fortunes. It is hard to tell who will be the winner and who will be the loser among the spinning wheels of Dharavi's business at the end of the day.

VIDJAY — IN THE LEATHER FACTORY

"I inherited this business from my grandfather who started it. I was born in Dharavi and have lived here all my life. Nowadays the hides come from Chennai but earlier the cattle were slaughtered here.

"We finish off raw hides and leather, manufacture leather belts and supply the clothing industry with leather patches for trousers and jeans. Our customers include brands like Macciavelli, Fubu, Dranila, H & M, Brandtex, Creative Garment and Lindex. We usually don't emboss the brand names on the leather here, it is done elsewhere. We don't make our own designs, never even took it into consideration, and in order to do that we would need more money and advertising. We are just a small industry providing for the needs of larger companies. Mostly we are contacted and keep in touch through the Internet or by networking.

"Most things are good in Dharavi. I don't like the way the media depicts us, I think they exploit us. It is not fair because we have good living standards and jobs. Of course the standard could be higher and hopefully it will develop. So far not much has happened but I am full of hope. I have 60 employees in my factory." *LE / ML*

4:56

4:55 Sunny Koshy runs the South Indian Chemical Trading Co, a company providing leather industries in Dharavi with chemicals. Sunny inherited the business from his father who started it. He lives with his two daughters in a middle class area north of Dharavi. Although it is Sunny's business to sell chemicals, he is very aware of the environment and tries to keep away from the most dangerous compounds. Sunny is also very critical of how the leather manufacturers are very indifferent to the situation of the workers who are heavily exposed to the chemicals. As an answer to the question of how to solve the problem, his answer is a resigning "it is all about business".

4:56 Vidjay inherited his business from his grandfather.

4:57 A businessman in plastic recycling. Bottles are turned into batting for duvets and filling for pillows, aimed at the European market.

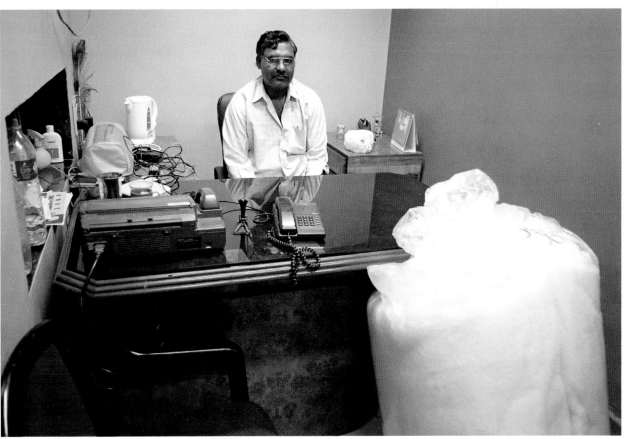

4:57

4:58

4:59

4:58   All sorts of plastic can be melted down and made into pellets. These pellets are then sold as fresh, new, raw material. It is both used in Dharavi and sold for export

4:59   The first step after stripping off the label from a water bottle, is to grind it into flakes. These flakes are the result of two water bottles being ground.

4:60   Locally produced sandals for sale.

4:61   Suitcases assembled and packed in Dharavi ready for export.

4:62   Some of the small things produced by recycled plastics in Dharavi, are the clips you find when buying underwear and shirts.

PRODUCTS

"You name it and Dharavi makes it". More things than you could possibly imagine are produced in the area. The things you see are often in various steps of processing – for instance leather and plastic of a certain quality can be specially made here. Highly advanced details for certain products such as the wheels on suitcases are exported to other countries where they fit into the production chain of well known brands. Other sophisticated products are made entirely in Dharavi, like embroided leather shoes.

ML / JHE

4:60

4:61

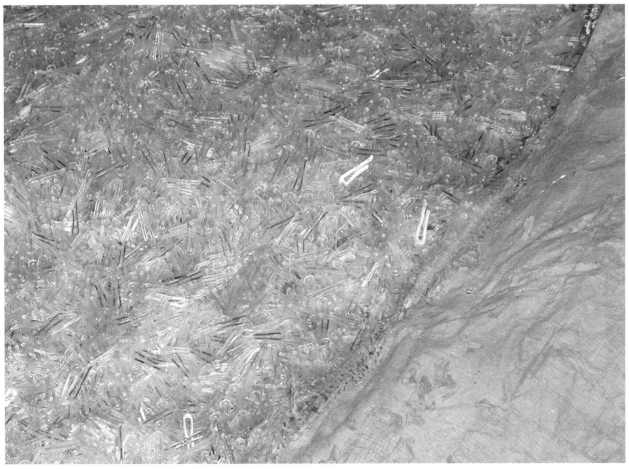

4:62

4:63

4:64

4:65

4:66

4:66

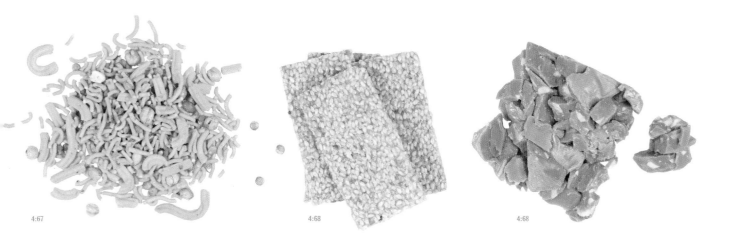

4:67

4:68

4:68

4:70

4:71

4:63 The leather patches on the back of a pair of jeans might very well be produced in Dharavi. When sent off on export, nothing is yet printed on the patch. The third patch shows what it can look like when it eventually has been printed. Here by the Swedish fashion brand H&M.

4:64 Plastic tags and hangers are made in Dharavi from recycled plastic.

4:65 Stickers for commercial advertisement and labelling. Made and printed locally.

4:66 The printing industry is connected to packaging. The simple boxes we throw away after taking out the component packaged inside, may be made in Dharavi. On the white box one can see the logotype of the Hong Kong Shanghai Banking Corporation, HSBC which is one of the largest banks in the world.

4:70 A "blank" CD used when packing CDs all over Asia, which are then exported all over the world. Again, the raw material comes from the recycling industry.

4:71 The plastic handle on a rolling suitcase made from recycled plastics. Handles, wheels and entire bags are made and assemled in Dharavi both for export and the local market.

4:67 Salty snacks fried with lentils and chick-peas.

4:68 Chiki is sold all over India – everywhere. It is a sweet that can contain sesame seeds, nuts and dry fruit. Chiki is made all over Dharavi for export to the rest of the city and further away.

How to make dry fruit chiki:

1 cup cashew
1 cup badam
1 cup pista
1/4 cup jaggery
2 spoons ghee
Kesar soaked in milk

1) Shred the jaggery into small pieces and melt ghee in a kadhai.
2) Place the grated jaggery in ghee and mix well to form fine paste.
3) Add cashew nuts, badam, kesar and pista and mix well.
4) Apply a layer of ghee in a tray and transfer the dry fruit mixture on to it.
5) Spread the mixture evenly and cool and divide it into pieces.

CHAPTER 5

FAMILY AND HOUSING

Home

It is impossible to describe the building style of Dharavi in one sentence. There are such a mix of different constructions and styles that it cannot be summarized. However, Dharavi could be described as a city of collaborative work, a monument to negotiation and innovation. The self built houses have been cantilevered over the alleys so that the upper floors stick out and meet over the narrow streets. Some parts of the city have no sanitation or just open sewers, yet other parts feel like villages in the countryside. Here and there high-rises stick up. The history of these buildings differ as much as the history of every self built house: some are built by private constructors, some are the result of people's organization in Dharavi who have managed to negotiate leaving their squatted homes in order to move into buildings with proper sanitation. By leaving land for private use, this has been sold and the money generated has been the base for constructing apartment buildings.

Compared to life in the formal and planned city, things in the informal sector can appear upside down. In formal society, one would take a loan, get a permit and then build a house. In Dharavi, one would start building, continue when money comes available and eventually claim a permit. This is why Dharavi keeps changing and keep being re-invented. Strange as it may seem, some of the squatters in Dharavi pay rent to the city of Mumbai, as in Squatters Colony, one of the nagars of Dharavi. The city collects money from these illegal residents, provides water and electricity, yet there is no sewage or other services found in the rest of the city.

Any family in Mumbai that can prove they have stayed in a place since before January 1, 1995, will be given a new home for free if their house is targeted for eviction. There is also something called a zoning bonus, which can be provided for private developers. This means the squatters can make a deal with a developer and sell their floor area for a density boost. If a high-rise can host 10 times as many floorratios there can be a win-win situation. However, there are always catches to ideas made in offices:

First of all, this ties squatters to the real estate market. The higher the prices on the market, the greater the value of the zoning bonus. But if prices fall, there is a risk in this game which many squatters are not willing to play.

Secondly, the floor area in the zoning system is set to 20.82 square metres, regardless of family size. Even if a house often occupies this size on the ground, there are often two or three floors. Some homes have managed to extend to 50 or more square metres. When this floorratio is moved up in a high-rise, the family only get one room to share. Not even a toilet and running water can make up for the loss of space. People simply cannot fit into the spaces offered.

Another problem is the lack of spaces to share and to produce things in. A lot of homes and the space outside are used for work, manufacturing, buying and selling. In the alleys life is lived, information shared, children can play. These activities are difficult to keep up with if you live on the 8th floor.

Moreover, the policy is not designed for tenants, the poorest squatters. If and when the self built houses are torn down to make place for apartment buildings, these people are simply forced to find new homes elsewhere.

As we will see, there are still ways to solve upgrading and the policies that the government have proposed are at least a step towards an understanding and an acknowledgement of the squatters. However, nothing can be done – formally or informally without negotiation involving the people who actually live and work in Dharavi.

ML

Housing Statistics

Statistics are just sets of information which have been counted and interpreted over time. It seems simple enough, but can be a tricky business. Some things are easy to measure, others tend to slip away, shrink or disappear as soon as you take out your ruler or calculator.

In informal areas, every effort from the official state to investigate whom, what and how much could be a threat. People are suspicious, usually with good reason. The purpose of mapping has to be clear and honest in order to get truthful figures.

There are also other difficulties when measuring the informal. By definition, informal life is a flux. Nothing is set; there is a constant change. A truthful figure one day could be a lie the next. For instance, there could be more people living in Dharavi during the monsoon season when people sublet their houses, or less during the harvest when people leave Dharavi to help their families in the countryside.

Therefore, in order to formalize the informal, the complexity of every figure needs to be taken into account.

The figures in this survey are therefore estimations. Some statistics come from the city of Mumbai, others from the University of Kamla Raheja Vidyanidhi Institute for Architecture who have worked closely with the local organizations in Dharavi and with the non governmental organization SPARC.

POPULATION

According to the government there are about 57,000 families who are eligible for rehabilitation or 285,000 people when multiplied by the average family size of five. However, there is no clear basis for this figure. Unofficial sources instead state that somewhere between 500,000 and 600,000 people live in Dharavi. This is a calculation based on rough count of structures done by grass root and non-governmental organizations. Since there is a mix of formal and informal housing in the area, the government figure might only be counting its formal residents. People who have contracts for their flats in high-rises and people who were the original inhabitants of the villages are among these formal citizens.

However, even in these houses there are sublettings and relatives staying who are not present in the statistics.

The rest of the population, Dharavi's informal residents, are even more difficult to count. Here, a person might officially reside in a village far away, in a place he or she has hardly been to. Subletting and housing within small scale industries is also common. So is staying in "hostels" where you have a temporary address, in many cases for several years.

Today the population of Mumbai is around 13 million. The population in Indian cities has increased by 500% since the country's independence in 1947. Some 35% of Mumbai's population live under the UN poverty line and half of the population live more or less outside the formal economy. In Mumbai, the richest city of India, half the population live in slums.

Mumbai is said to have a density of 29,500 people per square kilometre, making it one of the most densely populated cities in the world.

If there are 500,000 people in Dharavi, the incredible density of 285,000 people per square kilometre it is hard to comprehend – it means that Dharavi is about 5 times denser than Kwoun Tong, which is the most crowded part of Hong Kong, where the density level is 55,077 people per square kilometre or Manhattan which has 50,000 people per square kilometre.

Despite, or perhaps due to this density, there is not much unemployment. 85% of the residents are employed. Over 5000 small scale industries and 1,500 single room factories generate an estimated yearly turnover of half a billion US dollars. The 30 million dollar leather industry alone is said to employ 200,000 workers in Dharavi. Some of these workers come to Dharavi to work on a dily basis.   *ML*

FLOOR SPACE INDEX AND FLOOR AREA RATIO

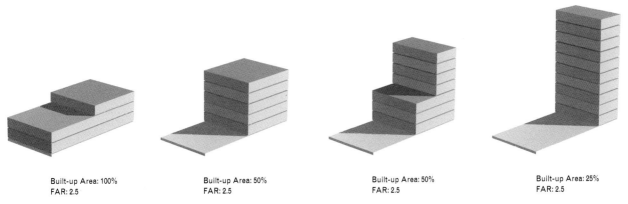

Built-up Area: 100%   Built-up Area: 50%   Built-up Area: 50%   Built-up Area: 25%
FAR: 2.5   FAR: 2.5   FAR: 2.5   FAR: 2.5

Floor Space Index (FSI) refers to the extent one can construct on a given plot of land. The calcultions can be related to the Floor Area Ratio (FAR) or Built-up Area index.

Re-location

GRASS ROOTS FOR BETTER HOUSING

One of the central infrastructures of Mumbai is the suburban commuter train. Many of the tracks are old and in the 1990s they were in need of urgent care. However, in certain parts of Mumbai the informal housing had come as close as one metre to the tracks. This forced trains to drive slowly and made maintenance of these lines impossible. The authorities were clearly troubled by this situation. Any attempt to actively deal with this situation would inherently involve the relocation of some twenty thousand households.

Informal as these households might be, many of them were and still are engaged in formal networks. People living along railway tracks, on pavements or by the roadside have become members of the National Slum Dwellers Federation (NSDF). Since the 1980s they have been investigating various strategies for community driven re-housing.

The NSDF has cooperated with the non-governmental organization Society for the Promotion of Area Resource Centres (SPARC) on several projects. When the discussions about expansion of the railway lines began, the two organizations presented a suggestion to the state government and to the railway federation. It was regarded as an impossible prospect mainly because of the informal settlements.

However, in 1998 some 800 families agreed to participate in a pioneering project. The families who lived along a stretch of central tracks offered to demolish their own homes, build transit homes themselves and organize there own move. In turn the government would provide land for them and the railway federation would provide financial assistance. The authorities did not need to exert force during the transitions and thanks to this community led method another 12 000 householders re-housed themselves during a second phase. This model has now been applied across other parts of India. Through contacts with the International Slum Dwellers International, it has served as an inspiration for organizations all over the world.

It is not by chance that these methods of organization have created successful results. The capacity of the community to organize itself, to plan and execute strategies in dialogue with the state is the key to the outcome of these projects.

In the case of the NSDF, for example, one important tool is the use of community led surveys. Details about individual households within a settlement are collected, verified and analysed by residents of this community. These surveys create a strong sense of "togetherness", but this is not the only purpose. Perhaps more importantly, the surveys allow the residents to come to a better understanding about the common issues held within their communities. When these issues become clear, common goals can be set up and "hard facts" formulated. These statistics are fundamental when negotiating with local authorities on the tenure of land, general resources and the improvement of living conditions.

Faced with highly organized community groups, there is no option for the municipalities but to take the voices of these organizations into consideration.

Poor men and women do not want to live on pavements, along railway tracks or in temporary shacks. But they cannot simply afford any other form of housing if they must live in the vicinity of their work.

Evictions have never been a healthy alternative and there are very few historical examples of successful large-scale resettlements in major cities. In Mumbai the municipalities have traditionally evicted all poor families living on the land that they want to exploit. In the few cases where the poor have been provided alternate land for resettlement, these areas are usually far from the city with poor water provision and little opportunity for work. The vast majorities of these resettled communities eventually return to more central parts of the city and build new homes.

Perhaps the NSDF and SPARC along with the micro credits provided by Mahila Milan demonstrate how underprivileged communities can become highly organized in order to negotiate with municipalities in a peaceful and sustainable manner.

JHE

"Good governance has 8 major characteristics. It is participatory, consensus oriented, accountable, transparent, responsive, effective and efficient, equitable and inclusive and follows the rule of law. It assures that corruption is minimized, the views of minorities are taken into account and that the voices of the most vulnerable in society are heard in decision-making. It is also responsive to the present and future needs of society."

WHAT IS GOOD GOVERNANCE?

Report by the United Nations Economic and Social Commission for Asia and the Pacific (UNESCAP).

"Do you know what good governance is for a poor woman who lives as a pavement dweller in Bombay? Good governance for her is nothing else than getting access to a toilet ... so she can defecate without fear of being watched by others."

SHEELA PATEL

Society for the Promotion of Area Resource Centres (SPARC).

Two Homes

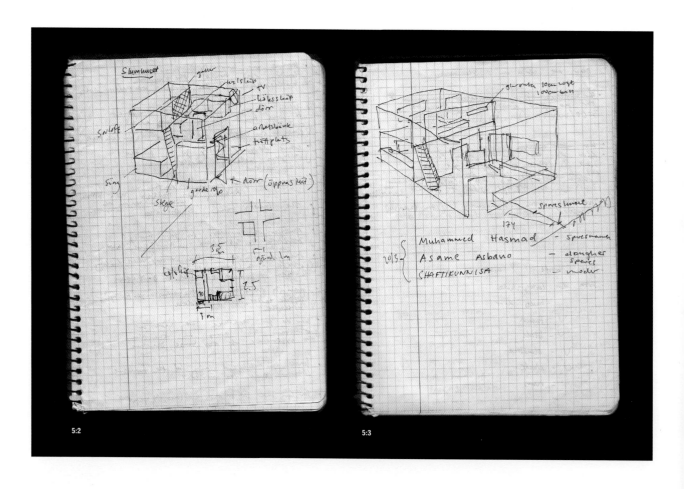

5:2   5:3

On the following pages we will look at two different homes in Dharvai. The first one, Shenaz's house, is situated in one of the most congested areas of Dharavi. It lies between Poonawalla Street, described earlier in this book, and Sion Link Road which runs along the border of Dharavi on the edge of the marsh.

The second home, Shafikunisa's house, is situated close to the first one but in a recently erected 6 floor high-rise apartment building. This building came about as a result of negotiations for land with the slum dweller's consent. Together with the non-governmental organization SPARC, local residents made a proposition to the city: by clearing off the shacks in the area, some of the land could be sold to private investors. The rest of the land could then be built on by those who left their houses. By placing the families on 8 floors instead of one or two, the families could gain some space. At the same time they would get their own kitchens and bathrooms.

The first home, Shenaz's house, will also be demolished in the near future. Instead, her family will gain a similar apartment to the one Shafikunisa's family has, in a similar building.

I wanted to compare a family living in the older, "slummier" part of Dharavi that is about to be demolished, with a family living in an apartment in the recently built SPARC building. I was interested to find out their thoughts about their living quarters and its relation to the other home. I formulated some basic questions as a foundation for a discussion with the families' mothers and as a background for my photographic documentation:

Who built your home?
How many members are there in your family?
Where do you eat and sleep?
What is your family origin? Do you come from Mumbai, India or elsewhere?
What are your neighbours and your own religious beliefs?
Where does your family go to have fun? Play, gamble, drink etc?
Do the children in your family study at school?
What is your family's primary occupation and income?
Does your family use any of the public spaces in the area?
Does your family walk the streets at nights?

Finally, I asked them about their relationship to the other home (in the SPARC building or in the slum) and what they would think of living in the other home. I also asked them if they had any thoughts on the future of Dharavi.   *MK*

5:2   Sketched plan of
       Shenaz's house with a
       floor space of approxi-
       mately 10 m².

5:3   Sketched plan of Shafi-
       kunisa's apartment.

5:4

SHENAZ'S HOUSE

Khan Jamal, Dusterwala, Kalyanwadi,
Tever Nagar, Dharavi, Sion Link Road,
Opp Sidra Hotel, Mumbai, India

The Shenaz family gets up at 6 in the morning. Her children go to school at 12.30. They do not go to the Mosque in the morning. They eat lunch around noon and dinner between 9 and 10 in the evening. After a short walk around 10, Shenaz goes to bed around 10.30. They live in a house built by Shenaz's grandfather. The family has lived there for 22 years. There are eight people in the family: Shenaz (32) her husband (40) mother, sister, and 4 children (three sons 18, 12, 6 and one daughter, 4). The family is Muslim and comes from Uttar Pradesh. There are two mosques nearby, their neighbours are Hindu and the children attend a Christian school.

The family's primary income comes from tailoring jeans and embroidery. The women work in the home and the common income is approximately 3,000 rupees per month.

They pay 100 rupees to the government office for electricity every month. They are not part of any micro-credit system or bank, but save on their own.

Shenaz says that it is safe to go outside at any time and even if she does not use public spaces much herself, the children often play in open spaces like the parking area close to the SPARC house.

The family sleeps both upstairs in the sleeping loft and downstairs. They eat their meals either on the floor or on the bed.

Shenaz thinks that the SPARC system with new higher buildings and transit camps is a good solution. She hopes to move to the transit area in about a year, even if it will cost them 1,000 rupees for a temporary home there. She thinks that there are good relations but no difference in status between the two homes even if she would like to get the same type of apartment as Shafikunisa as soon as possible.

5:4 This is the neighbourhood where Shenaz
lives. The photograph is
taken from the roof of
the SPARC building.

5:5   The narrow alley where
      Shenaz lives with her family.

5:6   Due to the lack of space
      indoors, laundry will be
      washed in the alley outside,
      where lighting and drainage
      conditions are better.

5:6

5:7

5:8

5:9

5:10

5:11

5:7 Regardless of how poor they are, most families own a relatively new TV-set. Following world events or watching entertainment programs is seen as an important part of daily leisure.

5:8 All the spaces in the home are used for specific purposes. On top of the kitchen cupboard, cooking vessels are piled to dry after being washed. The kitchen has portable gas burners and stainless steel cooking pots. Items that cannot be piled are hung up on hooks, using the little space available as effectively as possible.

5:9 Shenaz's youngest child is describing the monsoon. On the wall ... Traces of damage from the latest monsoon. Due to the low level of the house, water sometimes comes as high as a metre inside.

5:10 Since the home lacks windows and a ventilation system, an old table fan is placed by a barred opening for better ventilation. Next to the fan there is a religious Muslim image.

5:11 One of Shenaz's sons in front of the family's mirror, which is placed on the wardrobe door.

5:12

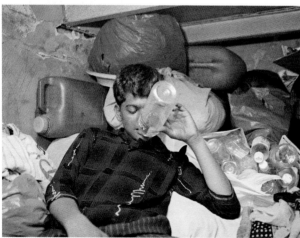

5:13

5:12   One of Shenaz's sons has got new glasses so that he can follow teaching better in school. He is sitting on the sleeping-loft. During the monsoon period this will be the only dry place in the home, filling all of the home's functions.

5:13   One of the neighbour's children is playing drunkard on the family's sleeping loft.
The sleeping loft is also one of the family's few storage areas where used plastic products are stored before they are sold to the local recycling industry.

5:14   Visiting relatives and friends proudly show off their newly purchased refrigerator. One gladly offers guests cold drinks of international brands like Coca-Cola.
The stainless steel plates and mugs are kept in bookshelf-like constructions that also function as a plate rack.

5:15

5:16

5:15 It is not unusual for house
owners to sublet the upper
floor of their home in order
to stabilise income. Tenants
commonly have an entrance of
their own by means of a step-
ladder outside the building.

5:16 The meter above the outer-
door tells the representatives
of the electric company how
much electricity the family
consumes.

5:17

5:17   The family's closest ladies' toilet is approximately 300 metres from their home. Since many people cannot read, there is a painted woman's head at the entrance.

5:18   The U.M. Thevar School, a Christian Elementary School where Shenaz's children study.

5:19   The men's toilet has a more open structure than the women's toilet.

5:20   The local mosque that Shenaz visits on a daily basis.

5:18

5:19

5:20

5:21

5:21

5:21   The parking lot in front of the
        new SPARC building is the
        only open public area. The
        children run around or play
        cricket there when it is not
        occupied by the builders – the
        parking lot is also a popular
        refuge for stray dogs.

5:21

5:21

5:21

SHAFIKUNISA'S APARTMENT

Asbano Hasmad, Dharavi Vikas Samethi, Kalyan Wadi, Tever Nagar, Sion Mahim Link Road, Mumbai, India.

Shafikunisa lives in an apartment in the SPARC building and says that the architect is A. Jockin, and that Parbu or Wasim are the construction company who built the house. They have lived there for four years and the rent is 300 rupees per month.

The family consists of nine people: Shafikunisa herself (50) her husband (60) her daughter (20) her son (35) and his wife (25) their cousin, and 3 children (7, 8 and 1 year old). Two of the children study at Makim Saint Michel School. The family originally comes from Alababa in Uttar Pradesh (in northern India) but their home traditions are mixed with the Mumbai way of life.

They eat on the floor downstairs. Sometimes they also eat together with the neighbours. Sahfikunisa and her husband sleep downstairs and the young couple sleeps upstairs.

Her husband and her son both work as leather tailors in a nearby leather factory. Their income is approximately 2000 rupees per person per month. They do not have savings in the bank and are not part in any micro credit system.

The family is Muslim and they regularly visit the Sunni Mosque nearby. Their neighbours are Hindus, Christians and Muslims. "We have no problem with this." says Shafikunisa. "You have to be friends when you live so close to each other. We even participate in their religious celebrations".

They are not afraid of the darkness and move freely in Dharavi, but they do not use the public areas much. The children do not use the roof or the yard but instead play inside the house. They also play in the alleyways and corridors since they lack regular playgrounds.

Before moving into this apartment they lived in the transit area for nearly four years. Shafikunisa says, it was a mess, with lots of problems. She seems content with their current living situation and thinks that their apartment looks cleaner than the other home.

What do you think of the future of Dharavi?

"It will not change. It is too costly. I have no ideas of the big plans for the future."

5:22 The SPARC building is in the
centre and Shafinisa's apartment is on the corner of the
third floor. There are several
new building sites in the area
and SPARC's is just one them.
In these buildings, families
that used to live in the slum
can mix with the middle class
inhabitants who are the main
tenants in Dharavi's other
high-rise projects.

5:23

5:23   Franzez Waza, the local
        security guard of the SPARC
        Building.

5:24   In the disorder that follows
        a building project, undefined
        areas have become assimi-
        lated by the local residents.
        A shady place like this is used
        partly as a transport route
        for the builders and also as
        a parking lot and a place to
        hang out.

5:25   The inner yard of the entrance,
        where Franzez Waza is station-
        ed. The yard is equipped with
        a blackboard, which children
        play with. All the windows
        have bar constructions which
        are used for drying laundry and
        dishes.

5:24

5:25

5:26 An informal parking lot for motorcycles in front of a sign giving information about a new SPARC Building.

5:27 Shafikunisa and her daughter together with the neighbouring children in the external gallery outside her apartment.

5:28 Images from the most common religious beliefs have been tiled in the corners of the stairwell to stop people from spitting or urinating there.

5:29 The stairwell is open and connected to the corridors and external galleries, giving light and fresh air as well as creating spaces for socialising and play.

5:27

5:28

5:29

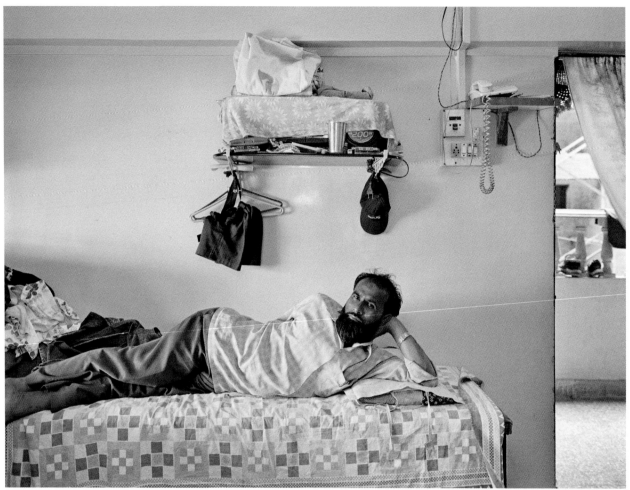

5:30

5:31

5:32

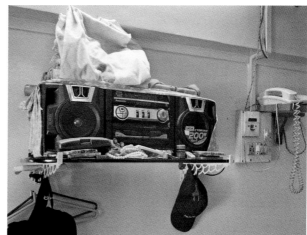

5:33

5:30 Muhammad Hasmad, Shafikunisa's relative, is resting
after his morning's work shift.
He is home for lunch and will
soon go back to work at the
leather factory.

5:31 The family's collection of
pictures with religious Muslim
motifs.

5:32 The apartment has one room, a
kitchen and a sleeping loft. The
beds are placed alongside the
walls of the apartment. Extra
mattresses and covers can be
rolled up and placed where
there is available space.

5:33 The family's newly purchased
stereo. The apartment is also
equipped with a telephone of
its own.

5:34 The ladder leading up to the
loft. The light, steel construc
tion makes it easy to get at
the space behind the ladder.
That space is used for storing
empty bottles of gas and a
hand-driven sewing machine.

5:34

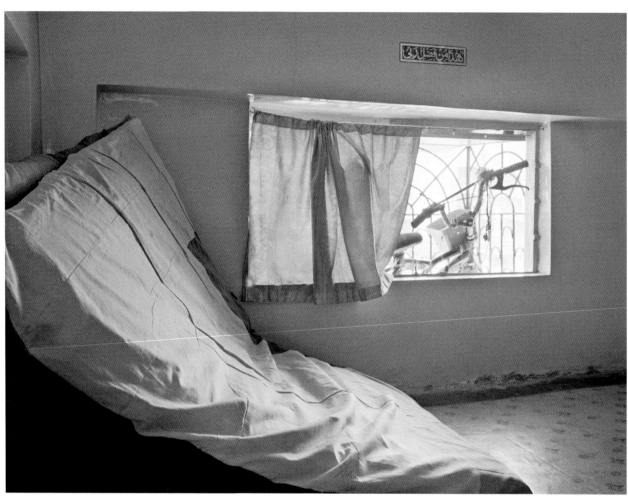

5:35

5:35   The ceiling is low above the
        sleeping loft, but there is
        enough space for Shafikunisa's
        son and his family. The chil-
        dren's bicycles are stored in the
        barred cage-like construction
        outside the window. To free up
        more space, all the mattresses
        are put away during the day.

5:36   The sleeping loft also has
        a wash basin of its own and
        sometimes it is also used as a
        toilet at night when the children
        are too tired to climb down the
        ladder.

5:36

5:37

5:38

5:38

5:37   The kitchen ceiling and the
       barred cage outside the
       window are used for hanging
       laundry and drying dishes.

5:38   The house has running water
       enabling a separate wash
       room and toilet.

5:39   The family's kitchen with its
       washing basin, gas stove,
       samovar and plate rack.

5:40   Shafikunisa between the door
       and the ladder that leads up to
       the sleeping loft.

5:41   (Next page.) The sunny roof of
       the building can be used for
       drying chilli or peas. The peo-
       ple who live in the surrounding
       area are not allowed to use the
       roof of the SPARC building.
       The roof is also ideal for hang-
       ing laundry. It is possible to tap
       water from the water cisterns.

5:39

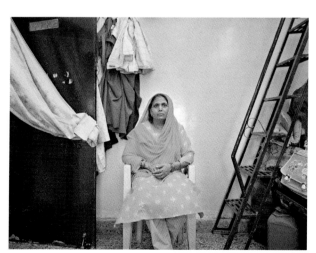

5:40

5:42

5:42 Kasturi Kadam is
talking to her beloved
grandson. Kasturi's
oldest daughter
Sandhya lives with her
family outside Dharavi.

The Kadam Family

– AN INTERVIEW WITH KASTURI KADAM

On our first trip to Dharavi we often met the Kadam family on our walks on Poonawalla. Coming back a year later, our friendship grew deeper and we were invited to spend time with the family. With great generosity, the Kadam family shared stories about their life, gains and drawbacks, their struggles and hopes for the future. We laughed, cried, made food and rested together in the blue interior of their apartment on Poonawalla.

KASTURI KADAM: My father and mother lived in Sion, and I was brought up in this area, the Dharavi-Sion area.

I was educated up to the 7th standard. My father died when I was studying at the 5th standard, and my older sister had to look after me and my family. My family arranged my marriage, and when I was 16 years old I married Devidas. By the age of 18 I had my first child, a daughter.

ANNA ERLANDSON / STINA EKMAN: Can you explain how your marriage was arranged?

KK: My father had a business before and his business partner said, "I have a son, will you give me one of your daughters?" I was looking nice then, so I was chosen from my two sisters they offered me and we got married. But then there was a life turn. After I had my first child, the story is very sad – crying and crying. At the beginning my husband was a good man, a businessman in leather work. The first five or six years he was very nice. We had a nice life, but after six years he lost his business.

AE / SE: Why?

KK: There was a quarrel between the business partners and because of the partner he lost the leather factory. After that he became a very heavy drunkard. The following years were very difficult to for me. My husband was always drunk, and he used to go early in the morning at four o'clock, to drink. When I was at work he came home, taking all the food from me and the children. He beat me often, so I always said to the children, "I am earning and my husband is sitting here and drinking up all the money so there is no use."

We where living together with Bhimsen family [Devidas's brother and his family of five people], but because of Devidas's drinking problems, and of all the quarrels and all the beatings, our families separated. Bhimsen said, "Move out." so our family moved out with the children to a place for rent. And at that time, I was the only one working, not my husband.

My youngest daughter Sarika was two years old at that time. So it's 15 years ago. You see, out of submission, I was doing work in a plastic industry, separating the plastic from all the garbage. That work I had to do. All day, from ten in the morning to ten at night. I was standing in water, sorting and washing out the plastic, garbage and all. I was doing full work.

At that time, my husband was always drunk and ate lots of food. There was hardly any food but he was eating all the food in the house. I earned sixteen rupees per day. Sixteen. One, six. Every day I was working hard for my family, allowing my husband to drink and daily I gave him five rupees to drink. I was doing very hard work at that time.

AE/SE: But how could you manage the whole family with just 16 rupees and a drunk husband?

KK: During this period, my father-in-law supported us. He came after 10 pm and he gave me 10 – 20 rupees per day saying, "Give this to your children, buy something for your children." My father-in-law was very supportive.

AE/SE: And you had five children?

KK: Yes, I had five children to manage, four daughters and one boy. So I was always looking here and there for more money. And when the first daughter was 15 – 16 years old, my husband's brothers, helped us with the marriage of our first daughter. After the first daughter's marriage I looked after the three daughters and the boy. I will always remember my great father-in-law. My mother-in-law was very aggressive and she did not want to help us, but my father-in-law always helped us.

My son, Atish, believed that his mother was suffering with all these problems, and that his father was not supporting us. Atish didn't want to stay with us. He went to stay somewhere else. My husband's brother took him in and gave him an education. And whenever my son came to me and asked for money, I took him to the plastic industry and the boss gave him some. My boss also helped us with the education of my son, Atish's education. He was very good. Because of my boss and my father-in-law I could manage, otherwise I would have collapsed.

My first daughter Sandhya, at the time when she was in 10th standard, when she was trying to study, my husband did not allow her to, saying, "Don't study, turn off the light, I want to sleep, don't study now." Although this happened, my daughter got her 10th standard and studied until the graduation and now, since two years back, she is married. Sandhya is very talented and she wanted to become a doctor. I said, "I don't have enough money to make you a doctor." I feel very bad now, to me my daughter is very talented but still we did not have the money to support her.

I suffered very much because of my husband being a drunkard. I always cried and cried and cried and my husband's brother said, "Don't cry, I will do something." So, my husband's brothers took Devidas to a centre in Pune where they tried to stop men from drinking, and after that my husband has never been drunk again.

AE/SE: And that was how many years ago?

KK: This was ten years ago.

AE/SE: But how is it to come back to someone you have to get to know again and build a new confidence with? How is that to come back to the person who has been doing so much damage and …?

KK: At that time when my husband was at the hospital, the doctor called me and said, "If you want to keep your husband sober you have to do one thing: don't allow him to eat meat and fish, because when he eats fish or meat, he will always remember the taste of alcohol." So we slowly stopped eating meat and fish. And I am feeling very good because now my husband is okay, though we are still suffering lots of things but one good thing is that my husband lives with me now and is in a very good condition.

AE/SE: Seeing you and Devidas together, it seems like you have something good in common, humour or something.

KK: Now, when my husband is in front of others, he always says that he is a very good man because of his wife – because of her help. Nowadays he appreciates me.

And he says, "Until your daughters get married, until then you are working. But after they are married you are staying at home and only I will work."

AE/SE: And Atish has come back home too? He's staying with the family now?

KK: Yes, Atish, yes.

AE/SE: Poonawalla Chawl seems to be an enclosed neighbourhood, if something happens, like a husband is falling out of the system, do other women around or other families support? How is it treated in the neighbourhood?

KK: Nobody was supporting us, no nobody was supporting … Only my father-in-law helped us, no one else.

AE/SE: So even though everyone can see when he is coming home drunk and falling around in the street, but no one is doing anything?

KK: He was not falling here and there, he was always drunk and came directly to me. If he had not eaten well, because of the alcohol, he would have died …

AE/SE: The house that you are living in, at Poonawalla Chawl, I understand that it belonged to Devidas's father. You moved out of there and moved in again, is that so?

KK: This room, now we are living in this room, it is now transferred to my husband. Before, it was in my father-in-law's name.

AE/SE: But last year when we were here, Bhimsen, Soni (the daughter of Bhimsen) and her mother were also living in the house?

KK: Last year we were all living together here, but now, there is a former workshop of my father-in-law, that the Bhimsen family is reconstructing. It has one room and Bhimsen and his family are living there now.

AE/SE: You will be giving away your daughter Anjali in marriage. How do you foresee your daughter's and your coming grand-children's future? Do you think Anjali will be happy?

KK: Her husband is very good and wealthy, he lives in Kolapur. Because I don't have anything for them, for Anjali. Anjali will get good a husband.

I was always wondering if there would be any peace in my life – and I think this is the time of peace now, because all of my daughters are getting married, our son Atish has a good job and he is staying in our house. My husband is not drunk now. It is very good, no? From that condition, this condition is very good.

AE/SE to interpreter Sangeeta: I guess that there are lots of things to ask, but in one sense, as she did speak out of her heart and we hardly asked any questions, I think that it's her story and that's very good because it has come out from her desire to speak.

SANGEETA: You see this is a typical story of a woman in India, in the slum streets. Most of the women are suffering these problems.

5:43

Anjali is the third of Kasturi and Devidas's five children. She is about to get married. It is not an arranged marrige, but a so called love marriage. Her future husband's name is Ratanakar, he is a businessman. After the wedding Anjali will move in to his big house in Kolapur, Maharashtra, far away from Mumbai. Kasturi's painful separation from her daughter is obvious. And even if Anjali is lucky to move into a big house with indoor wcs, she will be far away from the family. A traditional Indian wedding is an enormous arrangement, often with more than a thousand guests to feed. There are special wedding sites to rent that can fit in everyone along with cooks and serving staff. When a girl is born, a poor family knows what will come and they have to save money for a dowry and wedding costs.

Sony's real name is Purnima, but everyone calls her Sony. She is Sarika and Anjali's cousin but they are like sisters. Sony's father is Bhimsen, Devidas's brother.

Now that Sony and Anjali are getting married, life has taken a new turn. Sony's marriage was arranged by her parents. Her future husband's name is Santosh and he is an engineer working with oil platforms. He is middle class, and when they marry Sony will move to his parent's house, in a formal residential area far away from Dharavi. She becomes very shy when he suddenly shows up and it is clear that they do not know each other. Soon Sony will have to adjust to middle class life, and Santosh is paying for her english lessons.

AE/SE

5:43 From the left:
Sonys future husband
Santosh, Atish,
Devidas, Anjali, a
sister-in-law, Sarika, a
mother-in-law, Kasturi,
Sony and Sony's
mother.

5:44   After the family leather fac-
        tory closed, Devidas has a
        white collar job at the Golden
        Leather Works. Kasturi is
        working nights as an assisting
        nurse at Sion hospital.

5:45   Kasturi preforms the daily
        ritual by the house altar, the
        rituals are for the family
        ancestors and the gods. Atish
        is having lunch and resting at
        home. The family take turns
        resting during the daytime.

5:44

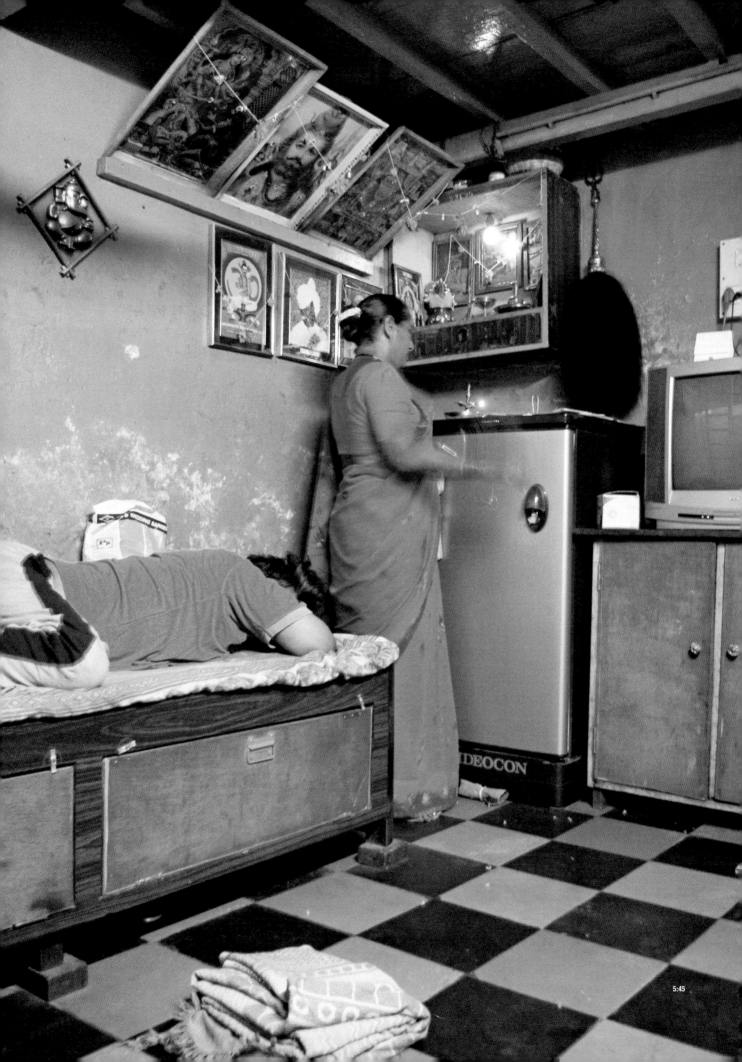

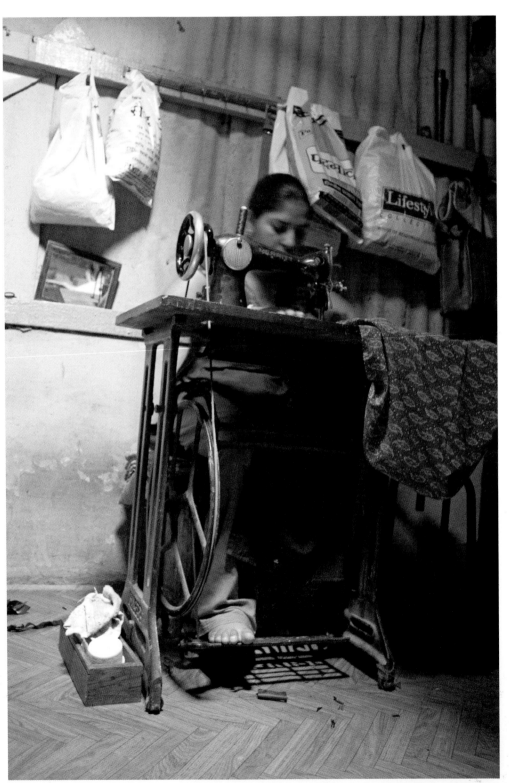

5:46

5:47

5:46 Anjali is very skilled in drawing and handicraft. She is sewing all the saris that the women of the family will wear when the weddings come. First it is Sony's wedding and four days later Anjali's. The preparations have been going on for a very long time.

5:47 Sony is drawing two hearts on her leg. Not only Sony's mind circulates around the topic of love and marriage. The modern Indian movie industry is now depicting young and passionate love in a more western fasion, confronting old values and pragmatism in classical love stories repeated in endless variations. There is a gap between the massive focus on love in mass media, and the fact that most Indian girls are facing a life with someone they have to get to know after they get married.

5:48

5:48

5:49

5:48   Sarika and Anjali are
        doing all the cooking.
        When they have left
        the house to live with
        their husbands families,
        Atish will marry a wom-
        an who will take over
        the responsibility for
        the household and its
        members. The tradition
        might be a necessity for
        many poor people as
        there is no communal
        care for the elderly.

5:49   Sarika is the youngest
        daughter. For a while
        she will take care of the
        household. Kasturi is
        looking for a husband
        for her.

5:50   Sony right before the
        wedding rituals start,
        dressed in her wedding
        sari.

5:51   Ratanakar and Anjali
        during their wedding
        ceremony.

5:50

5:51

"We usually say that we live in Mahim-East"

Roma, 24 and Riwa 18, speaking about living in the Vaibhav Apartments

Outside the ornamented iron gate that marks the border between Dharavi's labyrinth of alleys, and the blue and white high-rise on Dharavi Main Road, two boys are selling lemons from a cart. Next to them, a guard discretely lets traffic pass in and out of the enclosed area surrounding the Vaibhav Apartments. Here a Toyota, and there a dark and shiny Renault Twingo. Some people are on their way home for a quick lunch, others are starting the day with some shopping errands in Mumbai City.

The middle class families who live here have no interest in coming closer to the heart of Dharavi, through the winding walks among plastic recyclers, bakeries, waste handlers, tanners, an ocean of people. Many have installed themselves along the railway or by the enormous pipes that plough their way through fields of waste. The people who have moved into the Vaibhav Apartments did not do it in order to find out more about these informal settlements.

"We will say hi or hello, but we don't speak to them." This is how the sisters Roma and Riwa describe the lack of contact with people who live on the other side of the gate.

On New Year's Eve the neighbours sometimes arrange a common party on the roof terrace. The view from up there is almost surreal: shacks and corrugated roofs spread out over a radius of several kilometres. But when darkness falls the only light are the stars in the sky; there are no illuminated streets or homes. The ground below is pitch black and the Vaibhav Apartments are transformed into a luxurious craft without a compass on a dark and unknown sea. The modern, 14 floor building is a solitary island on the main street of Dharavi.

I walk through the blue iron gate and around the newly repainted high-rise, but do not experience it as an entrenchment. The gate serves as a border, a limit, but hardly as protection against intruders. The violent riots that took place in Dharavi during 1992 – 93 seem a world away. Children are making noise in the playground and servants pass in and out of the building's main entrance. A guard stops me and asks me who I am here to visit. I turn to a woman coming from the parking lot and when she hears that I am studying metropolitan areas of the world and am interested in the living conditions of Dharavi she invites me into the building.

"My husband is at his architectural office, but both of my daughters are at home" she says. Her name is Amita and she is an insurance salesman. "I am on a lunch break and have to get back soon, but there is time for a short conversation."

We take the elevator to the ninth floor. Amita and her family live in a two bedroom apartment with a living room, kitchen and bathroom. It is 85 square metres. The apartment's value has tripled during the fourteen years that they have lived in it. From a value of 1,200,000 Rupees (30,500 Euro) to 3,500,000 today (88,888 Euro) which, considering the average income in India, is a nauseating amount of money.

"It was very cheap when we bought it, but the area was also known as the largest slum in Asia." Amita says.

The family used to live in Chember, one of Mumbai's eastern satellite districts, but the trips to and from work were strenuous and so the move to Dharavi came as a relief.

5:53

The journey into town now takes half an hour by car or by train from Mahim station. But moving was a bold step for them to take and Amita wanted to get a good deal.

"Dharavi was not what it is today when we moved here in 1992, it was on the verge of improvement. At that time people thought Dharavi was a dangerous place. Rajiv Ghandi had announced the improvement of Dharavi. So through the municipality we found more out about this improvement plan. After that we bought the flat."

But it was not only Rajiv Ghandi's promises of massive funding of one hundred crore rupees [1,000,000,000 rupees or 25.4 million USD. 1 crore = 10 million rupees] that helped the family make their decission. Amita also talks about the developer K. Raheja in almost lyrical terms.

"This is the best builder in Mumbai and the company would never embark upon a project in a slum area of Dharavi's magnitude without a vision. Pretty early on we understood that competition would follow. Everything in our home has a high finish. Big windows and, yes, you can see it in every detail." Amita gestures towards the living room.

Builders, investors and real estate companies are all waiting for the social project in Dharavi to start rolling and for the slum to be removed. Everyone wants a slice of profits from the 600 eight story buildings that are planned on the land-filled marshlands of Dharavi.

But Amita sighs, "I have not encountered any difficulties living in Dharavi, despite what people say. But we never thought the improvements would happen so slowly. About five years ago I had plans to move from here. If I get an opportunity to buy a bigger flat with three bed rooms I will definitely move from Dharavi."

In her building all of the apartments are identical. No one has the three bedrooms that Amita dreams about. The family are watching the prices in the more attractive Mahim-West area, which in contrast to Mahim-East is not regarded as a part of Dharavi.

Amita's gaze wanders off, she excuses herself and sits down in front of the TV in her living room. Stocks are her passion and she watches the market's latest developments vigilantly. The conversation is passed on to her daughters, Roma, 24 and Riwa, 18. One of them qualified as a civil engineer in Cardiff, Wales, the other studies law at a college in Mumbai.

"Once we come home from college or town, we stay in." they say. "We never go out in Dharavi."

I ask them if they fear the area and they reply, "No, it is not that. The place is quite safe, even at night. But when we decide to see friends it would rather be roaming in good areas."

We start to talk about Dharavi as a cosmopolitan melting pot, with people from all four corners of India, different religions and "all that".

"Being in this building, staying for 14 years, I haven't gone inside Dharavi once. I only go from the station and I go by the main road. So I am not much involved in the area. I have a servant from Dharavi, that is all."

Roma and Riwa start giggling and say, "Usually we don't mention that we stay in Dharavi. We are pretty embarrassed about that, so we say we stay in Mahim-East. It is easier that way".

Mahim-East is next to a busy railway station and is a part of Dharavi. "We have told our parents to move from Dharavi a number of times but as it is now, it doesn't fit into their budget."

SA

The text is based on a conversation with Amita, Roma and Riwa, spring 2006.

5:52 (Page 245.) Vaibhav apartment, seen from outside the SPARC building

5:53 The blue iron gate outside the apartment building.

CHAPTER 6:

ORGANIZATION AND SUSTAINABILITY

Sustaining Ability

"On all sides we hear talk about the housing shortage, and with good reason. Nor is there just talk; there is action too. We try to fill the need by providing houses, by promoting the building of houses, planning the whole architectural enterprise. However hard and bitter, however hampering and threatening the lack of houses remains, the real plight of dwelling does not lie merely in a lack of houses."

MARTIN HEIDEGGER
"BUILDING DWELLING THINKING"

What does it means to dwell? Is it simply to find yourself a home somewhere? And what is it to be "at home"? A more elementary relationship to a place? Being at home cannot be reduced to living in a space that has or will become familiar. "To dwell" also means "to abide", "to reside", "to sustain", "to linger on", and also "to empathize". When thinking about sustainability, we must remember the importance of sustaining the resources that already exist on site. We must in a sense, "dwell" upon them.

In the following pages we present a few examples of people who are inventing new, sustainable solutions in their homes. Creating new solutions involves new negotiations and a re-thinking of old strategies. The grass root organizations that we have talked to are more than willing to negotiate on all levels. Of course they are generally in favour of a better functioning infrastructure, but what they want most of all is to use their voice to speak about the things they know. And one thing that people living in Dharavi know more than anyone else is the realities of life there. As we have seen earlier in this book, Mumbai was developed by a series of incremental negotiations. There can be no sustainability without listening to solutions which have already been supplied by the grass roots, without negotiating with those who have survived and flourished in Dharavi for many generations. *JHE*

6:1

Deep Democracy

URBAN GOVERNMENTALITY AND THE HORIZON OF POLITICS

by Arjun Appadurai

GLOBALIZATION FROM BELOW

Post-1989, the world seems marked by the global victory of some version of neoliberalism, backed by the ubiquitous presence of the United States and sustained by the common openness to market processes of regimes otherwise varied in their political, religious, and historical traditions. At the same time, more than a decade after the fall of the Soviet order, it is clearer than ever that global inequality has widened, intranational warfare has vastly outpaced international warfare (thus leading some observers to suggest the image of a Cold Peace), and various forms of violent ethnicization seem to erode the possibilities of sustainable pluralism. All this in a period that has also witnessed increased flows of financial capital across national boundaries and innovations in electronic communications and information storage technologies – the paradoxes abound, and have led to the proliferation of new theories of civilizational clash and of global gaps between safe and unsafe physical zones and geographical spheres. Fears of cyberapartheid mix with hopes for new opportunities for inclusion and participation.

In this confusion, now exacerbated by the knowledge that neither the most recent innovations in communications nor the defeat of the Soviet Union has created the conditions for global peace or equity, two great paradigms for enlightenment and equity seem to have become exhausted. One is the Marxist vision, in all its global variants, which promised some sort of politics of class-based internationalism premised on class struggle and the transformation of bourgeois politics by proletarian will. This is an internationalist vision that nevertheless requires the architecture of the nation-state as the site of effective struggle against capital and its agents. In this sense Marxism was, politically speaking, realist. The other grand vision, salient after 1945, was that of modernization and development, with its associated machinery of Western lending, technical expertise, and universalist discourses of education and technology transfer, and its target polity of the nationally based electoral democracy. This vision, born in such experiments as the Marshall Plan, has been subjected to intense criticism on numerous scores, but the starkest challenge to it is presented by the fact that today, over half a century after the Bretton Woods accords, more than half of the world's population lives in severe poverty.

In this context, a variety of other visions of emancipation and equity now circulate globally, often at odds with the nationalist imagination. Some are culturalist and religious, some diasporic and nonterritorial, some bureaucratic and managerial. Almost all of these recognize that nongovernmental actors are here to stay and somehow need to be made part of new models of global governance and local democracy.

The alliances and divisions in this new global political economy are not always easy to predict or understand. But among the many varieties of grassroots political movements, at least one broad distinction can be made. On the one hand are groups that have opted for armed, militarized solutions to their problems of inclusion, recognition, and participation. On the other are those that have opted for a politics of partnership – partnership, that is, between traditionally opposed groups, such as states, corporations, and workers. The alliance of housing activists whose story occupies the bulk of this essay belongs to the latter group and is part of the emergent process through which the physics of globalization is being creatively redeployed.

THE STORY

What follows is a preliminary analysis of an urban activist movement with global links. The setting is the city of Mumbai, in the state of Maharashtra, in western India. The movement consists of three partners and its history as an alliance goes back to 1987. The three partners have different histories. The Society for the Protection of Area Resource Centres, or SPARC, is an NGO formed by social work professionals in 1984 to work with problems of urban poverty in Mumbai. NSDF, the National Slum Dwellers' Federation, is a powerful grassroots organization established in 1974 and is a CBO, or community-based organization, that also has its historical base in Mumbai. Finally, Mahila Milan is an organization of poor women, set up in 1986, with its base in Mumbai and a network throughout India, which is focused on women's issues in relation to urban poverty and concerned especially with local and self-organized savings schemes among the very poor. All three organizations, which refer to themselves collectively as the Alliance, are united in their concern with gaining secure tenure of land, adequate and durable housing, and access to elements of urban infrastructure, notably to electricity, transport, sanitation, and allied services. The Alliance also has strong links to Mumbai's pavement dwellers and to its street children, whom it has organized into an organization called Sadak Chaap (Street Imprint), which has its own social

and political agenda. Of the six or seven nonstate organizations working directly with the urban poor in Mumbai, the Alliance has by far the largest constituency, the highest visibility in the eyes of the state, and the most extensive networks in India and elsewhere in the world.

This essay is an effort to understand how this came to be by looking at the horizon of politics created by the Alliance and by seeing how it has articulated new relations to urban governmentality. It is part of a larger ongoing study of how grassroots movements are finding new ways to combine local activism with horizontal, global networking. It is also, methodologically speaking, a partial effort to show how the anthropological study of globalization can move from an ethnography of locations to one of circulations. In my conclusion, I use the story of this particular network to discuss why it is useful to speak of "deep democracy" as a concept of wider potential use in the study of globalization.

THEORETICAL POINTS OF ENTRY

Three theoretical propositions underlie this presentation of the story of the Alliance in Mumbai.

First I assume, on the basis of my own previous work (Appadurai 1996, 2000, 2001) and that of several others from a variety of disciplinary perspectives (Castells 1996; Giddens 2000; Held 1995; Rosenau 1997), that globalization is producing new geographies of governmentality. Specifically, we are witnessing new forms of globally organized power and expertise within the "skin" or "casing" of existing nation-states (Sassen 2000). One expression of these new geographies can be seen in the relationship of "cities and citizenship" (Appadurai and Holston 1999), in which wealthier "world-cities" increasingly operate like city-states in a networked global economy, increasingly independent of regional and national mediation, and where poorer cities – and the poorer populations within them – seek new ways to claim space and voice. Many large cities like Mumbai display the contradictions between these ideal types and combine high concentrations of wealth (tied to the growth of producer services) and even higher concentrations of poverty and disenfranchisement. Movements among the urban poor, such as the one I document here, mobilize and mediate these contradictions. They represent efforts to reconstitute citizenship in cities. Such efforts take the form, in part, of what I refer to as deep democracy.

Second, I assume that the nation-state system is undergoing a profound and transformative crisis. Avoiding here the sterile terms of the debate about whether or not the nation-state is ending (a debate to which I myself earlier contributed), I nevertheless wish to affirm resolutely that the changes in the system are deep, if not graspable, as yet, in a simple theory. I suggest that we see the current crisis as a crisis of redundancy rather than, for example, as one of legitimation (Habermas 1975). By using the term redundancy, I mean to connect several processes that others have identified with different states and regions and in different dimensions of governance. Thus, in many parts of the world, there has been undoubted growth in a "privatization" of the state in various forms, sometimes produced by the appropriation of the means of violence by nonstate groups. In other cases, we can see the growing power in some national economies of multilateral agencies such as the World Bank and International Monetary Fund, sometimes indexed by the voluntary outsourcing of state functions as part of the neoliberal strategies that have become popular worldwide since 1989. In yet other cases, activist NGOs and citizens' movements have appropriated significant parts of the means of governance.

Third, I assume that we are witnessing a notable transformation in the nature of global governance in the explosive growth of nongovernment organizations of all scales and varieties in the period since 1945, a growth fueled by the linked development of the United Nations system, the Bretton Woods institutional order, and especially the global circulation and legitimation of the discourses and politics of "human rights." Together, these developments have provided a powerful impetus to democratic claims by nonstate actors throughout the world. There is some reason to worry about whether the current framework of human rights is serving mainly as the legal and normative conscience – or the legal-bureaucratic lubricant – of a neoliberal, marketized political order. But there is no doubt that the global spread of the discourse of human rights has provided a huge boost to local democratic formations. In addition, the combination of this global efflorescence of nongovernmental politics with the multiple technological revolutions of the last fifty years has provided much energy to what has been called "cross-border

activism" through "transnational advocacy networks" (Keck and Sikkink 1998). These networks provide new horizontal modes for articulating the deep democratic politics of the locality, creating hitherto unpredicted groupings: examples may be "issue-based" – focused on the environment, child labor, or AIDS – or "identity-based" – feminist, indigenous, gay, diasporic. The Mumbai-based movement discussed here is also a site of such cross-border activism.

Together, these three points of entry allow me to describe the Mumbai Alliance of urban activists as part of an emergent political horizon, global in its scope, that presents a post-Marxist and postdevelopmentalist vision of how the global and the local can become reciprocal instruments in the deepening of democracy.

THE SETTING: MUMBAI IN THE 1990s

I have recently completed a lengthy examination of the transformation of Mumbai's cultural economy since the 1970s, with an emphasis on the brutal ethnic violence of December 1992–January 1993 (Appadurai 2001). That essay contains a relatively detailed analysis of the relationships between the politics of right-wing Hindu nationalism – seen mostly in the activities of India's major urban xenophobic party, the Shiva Sena – the political economy of deindustrialization, and the spectral politics of housing in Mumbai. I analyze the steady expansion of anti-Muslim politics by the Shiva Sena, the radical inequality in access to living space in the city, and the transformation of its industrial economy into a service economy. I argue that Mumbai became a perfect site for the violent rewriting of Muslims from its public sphere and its commercial world.

I will not retell that story here, but I will review some major facts about Mumbai in the 1990s that are not widely known. Mumbai is the largest city in a country, India, whose population has just crossed the 1 billion mark (one-sixth of the world's population). The city's population is at least 12 million (more, if we include the growing edges of the city and the population of the twin city, New Mumbai, that has been built across Thane Creek). This means a population totaling 1.2 percent of one-sixth of the world's population. Not a minor case, even in itself.

Here follow some facts about housing in Mumbai on

which there is a general consensus. About 40 percent of the population (about 6 million persons) live in slums or other degraded forms of housing. Another 5 to 10 percent are pavement dwellers. Yet according to one recent estimate, slum dwellers occupy only 8 percent of the city's land, which totals about 43,000 hectares. The rest of the city's land is either industrial land, middle- and high-income housing, or vacant land in the control of the city, the state (regional and federal), or private owners. The bottom line: 5 to 6 million poor people living in substandard conditions in 8 percent of the land area of a city smaller than the two New York City boroughs of Manhattan and Queens. This huge and constricted population of insecurely or poorly housed people has negligible access to essential services, such as running water, electricity, and ration cards for food staples.

Equally important, this population – which we may call citizens without a city – is a vital part of the urban workforce. Some of them occupy the respectable low end of white-collar organizations and others the menial low end of industrial and commercial concerns. But many are engaged in temporary, physically dangerous, and socially degrading forms of work. This latter group, which may well comprise 1 to 2 million people in Mumbai, is best described, in the striking phrase of Sandeep Pendse (1995), as Mumbai's "toilers" rather than as its proletariat, working class, or laboring classes – all designations that suggest more stable forms of employment and organization. These toilers, the poorest of the poor in the city of Mumbai, work in menial occupations (almost always on a daily or piecework basis). They are cart pullers, ragpickers, scullions, sex workers, car cleaners, mechanic's assistants, petty vendors, small-time criminals, and temporary workers in petty industrial jobs requiring dangerous physical work, such as ditch digging, metal hammering, truck loading, and the like. They often sleep in (or on) their places of work, insofar as their work is not wholly transient in character. While men form the core of this labor pool, women and children work wherever possible, frequently in ways that exploit their sexual vulnerability. To take just one example, Mumbai's gigantic restaurant and food-service economy is almost completely dependent on a vast army of child labor.

Housing is at the heart of the lives of this army of toilers. Their everyday life is dominated by ever-present forms of risk. Their temporary shacks may be demolished. Their slumlords may push them out through force or extortion. The torrential monsoons may destroy their fragile shelters and their few personal possessions. Their lack of sanitary facilities increases their need for doctors to whom they have limited access. And their inability to document their claims to housing may snowball into a general invisibility in urban life, making it impossible for them to claim any rights to such things as rationed foods, municipal health and education facilities, police protection, and voting rights. In a city where ration cards, electricity bills, and rent receipts guarantee other rights to the benefits of citizenship, the inability to secure claims to proper housing and other political handicaps reinforce each other. Housing – and its lack – set the stage for the most public drama of disenfranchisement in Mumbai. In fact, housing can be argued to be the single most critical site of this city's politics of citizenship.

This is the context in which the activists I am working with are making their interventions, mobilizing the poor and generating new forms of politics. The next three sections of this essay are about various dimensions of this politics: its vision, its vocabularies, and its practices.

THE POLITICS OF PATIENCE

In this section, I give a sketch of the evolving vision of the Alliance of sparc, Mahila Milan, and the National Slum Dwellers' Federation as it functions within the complex politics of space and housing in Mumbai. Here, a number of broad features of the Alliance are important.

First, given the diverse social origins of the three groups that are involved in the Alliance, their politics awards a central place to negotiation and consensus-building. sparc is led by professionals with an anglophone background, connected to state and corporate elites in Mumbai and beyond, with strong ties to global funding sources and networking opportunities. However, sparc was born in 1984 in the specific context of work undertaken by its founders – principally a group of women trained in social work at the Tata Institute for the Social Sciences – among poor women in the neighborhood of Nagpada. This area has a diverse ethnic population and is located between the wealthiest parts of South Mumbai and the increasingly difficult slum areas of Central and North Mumbai.

Notable among SPARC's constituencies was a group of predominantly Muslim ex–sex trade workers from Central Mumbai who later became the cadre of another partner in the Alliance, Mahila Milan. The link between the two organizations dates to around 1986, when Mahila Milan was founded, with support from SPARC.

The link with the NSDF, an older and broader-based slum dwellers' organization, was also made in the late 1980s. The leadership of the three organizations cuts across the lines between Hindus, Muslims, and Christians and is explicitly secularist in outlook. In a general way, SPARC contributed technical knowledge and elite connections to state authorities and the private sector. NSDF, through its leader, Arputham Jockin (who himself has a background in the slums), and his activist colleagues, brought a radical brand of grassroots political organization in the form of the "federation" model, to be discussed later in this essay. Mahila Milan brought the strength of poor women who had learned the hard way how to deal with police, municipal authorities, slumlords, and real estate developers on the streets of Central Mumbai but had not previously had a real incentive to organize politically.

These three partners still have distinct styles, strategies, and functional characteristics. But they are committed to a partnership based on a shared ideology of risk, trust, negotiation, and learning among their key participants. They have also agreed upon a radical approach to the politicization of the urban poor that is fundamentally populist and anti-expert in strategy and flavor. The Alliance has evolved a style of pro-poor activism that consciously departs from earlier models of social work, welfarism, and community organization (an approach akin to that pioneered by Saul Alinsky in the United States). Instead of relying on the model of an outside organizer who teaches local communities how to hold the state to its normative obligations to the poor, the Alliance is committed to methods of organization, mobilization, teaching, and learning that build on what poor persons already know and understand. The first principle of this approach is that no one knows more about how to survive poverty than the poor themselves.

A crucial and controversial feature of this approach is its vision of politics without parties. The strategy of the Alliance is that it will not deliver the poor as a vote bank to any political party or candidate. This is a tricky business

in Mumbai, where most grassroots organizations, notably unions, have a long history of direct affiliation with major political parties. Moreover, in Mumbai, the Shiva Sena, with its violent, street-level control of urban politics, does not easily tolerate neutrality. The Alliance deals with these difficulties by working with whoever is in power, at the federal and state level, within the municipality of Mumbai, or even at the local level of particular wards (municipal subunits). Thus the Alliance has elicited hostility from other activist groups in Mumbai for its willingness, when deemed necessary, to work with the Shiva Sena. But it is resolute about making the Shiva Sena work for its ends, not vice versa. Indeed, because it has consistently maintained an image of nonaffiliation with all political parties, the Alliance enjoys the double advantage of appearing nonpolitical while retaining access to the potential political power of the poorer half of Mumbai's population.

Instead of finding safety in affiliation with any single party or coalition in the state government of Maharashtra or the Municipal Corporation of Mumbai, the Alliance has developed a complex political affiliation with the various levels of the state bureaucracy. This group includes civil servants who conduct policy at the highest levels in the state of Maharashtra and run the major bodies responsible for housing loans, slum rehabilitation, real estate regulation, and the like. The members of the Alliance have also developed links with quasi-autonomous arms of the federal government, such as the railways, the Port Authority, and the Bombay Electric Supply and Transport Corporation, and with the municipal authorities who control critical elements of the infrastructure, such as the regulations governing illegal structures, the water supply, and sanitation. Finally, the Alliance works to maintain a cordial relationship with the Mumbai police – and at least a hands-off relationship with the underworld, which is deeply involved in housing finance, slum landlordism, and extortion as well as in the demolition and rebuilding of temporary structures.

From this perspective, the politics of the Alliance is a politics of accommodation, negotiation, and long-term pressure rather than of confrontation or threats of political reprisal. This realpolitik makes good sense in a city like Mumbai, where the supply of scarce urban infrastructure – housing and all its associated entitlements – is entangled in an immensely complicated web of slum rehabilitation projects, financing procedures, legislative precedents, and administrative codes which are interpreted differently, enforced unevenly, and whose actual delivery is almost always attended by an element of corruption.

This pragmatic approach is grounded in a complex political vision about means, ends, and styles that is not entirely utilitarian or functional. It is based on a series of ideas about the transformation of the conditions of poverty by the poor in the long run. In this sense, the figure of a political horizon is meant to point to a logic of patience, of cumulative victories and long-term asset building, that is wired into every aspect of the activities of the Alliance. The Alliance maintains that the mobilization of the knowledge of the poor into methods driven by the poor and for the poor is a slow and risk-laden process; this premise informs the group's strong bias against "projects" and "projectization" that underlies almost all official ideas about urban change. Whether the World Bank, most Northern donors, the Indian state, or other agencies, most institutional sources of funding are strongly biased in favor of the "project" model, in which short-term logics of investment, accounting, reporting, and assessment are regarded as vital. The Alliance has steadfastly advocated the importance of slow learning and cumulative change against the temporal logics of the project. Likewise, other strategies and tactics are also geared to long-term capacity building, the gradual gaining of knowledge and trust, the sifting of more from less reliable partners, and so on. This open and long-term temporal horizon is a difficult commitment to retain in the face of the urgency, and even desperation, that characterize the needs of Mumbai's urban poor. But it is a crucial normative guarantee against the ever-present risk, in all forms of grassroots activism, that the needs of funders will gradually obliterate the needs of the poor themselves.

Patience as a long-term political strategy is especially hard to maintain in view of two major forces. One is the constant barrage of real threats to life and space that frequently assail the urban poor. The most recent such episode was the massive demolition of shacks near the railroad tracks, which, since April 2000, has produced an intense struggle for survival and political mobilization in the midst of virtually impossible circumstances that at the time of this writing had yet to be resolved. In this sense, the strategies of the Alliance, which favor long-term asset building, run against the same "tyranny of emergency," in the words of Jérôme Bindé (2000), that characterizes the everyday lives of the urban poor.

The other force that makes patience hard to maintain is the built-in tension within the Alliance about different modes and methods of partnership. Not all members of the Alliance view the state, the market, or the donor world in the same way. Thus, every new occasion for funding, every new demand for a report, every new celebration of a possible partnership, every meeting with a railway official or an urban bureaucrat can create new sources of debate and anxiety within the Alliance. In the words of one key Alliance leader, negotiating these differences, rooted in deep diversities in class, experience, and personal style, is like "riding a tiger." It would be a mistake to view the pragmatic way in which all partnerships are approached by the Alliance as a simple politics of utility. It is a politics of patience, constructed against the tyranny of emergency.

To understand how this broad strategic vision is actually played out as a strategy of urban governmentality, we need to look a little more closely at some critical practices, discursive and organizational, by which the Alliance has consolidated its standing as a pro-poor movement in Mumbai.

WORDS AND DEEDS

As with all serious movements concerned with consciousness-changing and self-mobilization, there is a conscious effort to inculcate protocols of speech, style, and organizational form within the Alliance. The coalition cultivates a highly transparent, nonhierarchical, antibureaucratic, and antitechnocratic organizational style. A small clerical staff conscientiously serves the needs of the activists, not vice versa; meetings and discussions are often held with everyone sitting on mats on the floor. Food and drink are shared during meetings, and most official business (on the phone or face-to-face) is held in the midst of a tumult of other activities in crowded offices. A constant undercurrent of bawdy humor runs through the members' discussions of problems, partners, and their own affairs. Conversation is almost always in Hindi, Marathi, or Tamil, or in English interspersed with one of these Indian languages. The leadership is at pains to make its ideas known among its members and to the residents of the actual slum communities who are, in effect, the coalition's rank and file. Almost no internal request for information about the organization, its funding, its planning, or related matters is considered out of order. Naturally, there are private conversations, hidden tensions, and real differences of personality and strategy at all levels. But these are not validated or legitimated in bureaucratic protocols or organizational charts.

This style of organization and management produces constant tensions among members of the Alliance and various outside bodies – donors, state institutions, regulators – which frequently demand more formal norms of organization, accounting, and reporting. To a very considerable extent the brunt of this stress is borne by SPARC, which has an office in Central Mumbai where the formal bureaucratic links to the world of law, accountancy, and reporting are largely centralized. This office serves partly to insulate the other two partners, NSDF and Mahila Milan, from the needs of externally mandated bookkeeping, fund management, reporting, and public legal procedures. The latter two organizations have their own headquarters in the compound of a municipal dispensary in Byculla. This office is in the heart of a slum world where many of the core members of Mahila Milan actually live, an area in which Muslims are a major presence, and the sex trades, the criminal world, and petty commerce are highly visible. The office is always filled with men and women from the communities of slum dwellers that are the backbone of the Alliance. There is constant movement among key personnel between this office, the SPARC office in Khetwadi, and the outlying new suburbs where the Alliance is building transit facilities or new houses for its members – Dharavi, Mankhurd, and Ghatkopar.

The phones are in constant use as key members of the Alliance exchange information about breaking crises, plans, and news across these various locations in Mumbai – and also across India and the world. Every few hours during an average day, a phone rings at one of these offices and turns out to be one of the members of the Alliance checking on or tracking down something – a call is as likely to come from Phnom Penh or Cape Town as from Mankhurd or Byculla. Because everyday organizational life is filled with meetings with contractors, lawyers, state officials, and politicians as well as among Alliance members, spatial fixity is not valued and the organization functions in and through mobility. In this context, the telephone and e-mail play an increasingly vital role. The key leaders of the Alliance, with a few significant exceptions, either use e-mail or have access to it through close colleagues. The phones are constantly ringing. Schedules shift at the drop of a hat as travel plans are adjusted to meet emergent opportunities or to address the presence or absence of key members. The general impression is of a fast game of ice hockey, with players constantly tumbling in and out of the most active roles in response to shifting needs and game plans.

Nevertheless, through experiences and discussions that have evolved over fifteen years (and, in some cases, more), there is a steady effort to remember and reproduce certain crucial principles and norms that offset organizational fluidity and the pressures of daily crises. These norms and practices require a much more detailed discussion than I can give in the current context, but some impression of them is vital to understanding the political horizon of this form of deep democracy.

Possibly the central norm is embodied in a common usage among the members of the Alliance and its partners around the world. It is the term federation, used as a noun, or federate and federated, used as verbs. This innocuous term from elementary political science textbooks has a special meaning and magic for the Alliance. At its foundation is the idea of individuals and families self-organizing as members of a political collective to pool resources, organize lobbying, provide mutual risk-management devices, and confront opponents, when necessary. Members of the Alliance often judge the effectiveness of other NGOs, in India and elsewhere, by reference to whether or not they have learned the virtues of federating. The National Slum Dwellers' Federation is clearly their own model of this norm. As an image of organization, it is significant in two ways. It emphasizes the importance of political union among already preexisting collectives (thus federating, rather than simply uniting, joining, and lobbying). And it mirrors the structure of the Indian national state, which is referred to as the Indian Union, but is in fact a federal model whose constituent states retain extensive powers.

In the usage of the Alliance, the idea of federation is a constant reminder that groups (even at the level of families) that have a claim to political agency on their own have chosen to combine their political and material power. The primacy of the principle of federation also serves to remind all members, particularly the trained professionals, that the power of the Alliance lies not in its donors, its technical expertise, or its administration, but in the will to federate among poor families and communities. At another level, the image of the federation asserts the primacy of the poor in driving their own politics, however much others may help them to do so. There is a formal property to membership in the federation, and members of the Alliance maintain ongoing debates about recruiting slum families, neighborhoods, and communities in Mumbai (and elsewhere in India) that are not yet part of the federation. For as long as the latter remain outside, they cannot participate in the active politics of savings, housing, resettlement, and rehabilitation that are the bread and butter of the Alliance.

Savings is another term that takes on a special meaning in Alliance usage. Creating informal savings groups among the poor – a process that the donor establishment has recognized under the term microcredit – is a current technique for improving financial citizenship for the urban and rural poor throughout the world. Often building on older models of revolving credit and loan facilities that are managed informally and locally, outside the purview of the state and the banking sector, microcredit has its advocates and visionaries in India and elsewhere. But in the life of the Alliance, savings has a profound ideological, even salvational, status. The architect of the Alliance philosophy of savings is the NSDF's Jockin, who has used savings as a principal tool for mobilization in India and as an entry point to relationship building in South Africa, Cambodia, and Thailand. He sees daily savings as the bedrock of all federation activities; indeed, it is not an exaggeration to say that in Jockin's organizational exhortations, wherever he goes, federation equals savings. When Jockin and his colleagues in the Alliance speak about savings, it becomes evident that they are describing something far deeper than a simple mechanism for meeting daily monetary needs and sharing resources among the poor. Seen by them as something akin to a spiritual practice, daily savings – and its spread – is conceived as the key to the local and global success of the federation model.

In this connection, it may be noted that Mahila Milan,

the women's group within the Alliance, is focused almost entirely on organizing small savings circles. By putting savings at the core of the politics of the Alliance, its leaders are making the work of poor women fundamental to what can be achieved in every other area. It is a simple formula: Without poor women joining together, there can be no savings. Without savings, there can be no federating. Without federating, there is no way for the poor themselves to enact change in the arrangements that disempower them. What is important to recognize here is that when Alliance leaders speak about a way of life organized around the practice of saving – in Jockin's words, it is like "breathing" – they are framing saving as a moral discipline. The practice builds a certain kind of political fortitude and commitment to the collective good and creates persons who can manage their affairs in many other ways as well. Daily savings, which do not generate large resources quickly, can therefore form the moral core of a politics of patience.

A final key term that recurs in the writing and speech of the leaders of the Alliance is precedent-setting. I am still exploring the ramifications of this strategic locution. What I have learned so far is that underlying its bland, quasi-legal tone is a more radical idea: that the poor need to claim, refine, and define certain ways of doing things in spaces they already control and then use these practices to show donors, city officials, and other activists that their "precedents" are good ones and encourage such actors to invest further in them. This is a politics of show-and-tell, but it is also a philosophy of do first, talk later. The subversive feature of this principle is that it provides a linguistic device for negotiating between the legalities of urban government and the "illegal" arrangements to which the poor almost always have to resort, whether the illegality in question pertains to structures, living strategies, or access to water, electricity, or anything else that has been successfully siphoned out of the material resources of the city.

Precedent-setting moves practices such as these, along with new techniques for accessing food, health services, police protection, and work opportunities, into a zone of quasi-legal negotiation. By invoking the concept of precedent as enshrined in English common law, the linguistic device shifts the burden for municipal officials and other experts away from a dubious whitewashing of illegal activities to a building on "legitimate" precedents. The linguistic strategy of precedent-setting thus turns the survival tactics and experiments of the poor into sites for policy innovations by the state, the city, donor agencies, and other activist organizations. It is a strategy that moves the poor into the horizon of legality on their own terms. Most important, it invites risk-taking activities by bureaucrats within a discourse of legality, allowing the boundaries of the status quo to be pushed and stretched – it creates a border zone of trial and error, a sort of research and development space within which poor communities, activists, and bureaucrats can explore new designs for partnership.

But the world is not changed through language alone. These key words (and many other linguistic strategies not discussed here) can be positioned as the nervous system of a whole body of broader technical, institutional, and representational practices that have become signatures of the Alliance's politics. Here, I will briefly discuss three vital organizational strategies that illustrate the ways in which technical practices are harnessed to the Alliance's political horizon. They are: self-surveys and enumeration; housing exhibitions; and toilet festivals.

Contemporary scholars, led by Michel Foucault, have drawn attention to the use of censuses and other techniques of enumeration by political regimes from the seventeenth century onward; Foucault and others have indeed observed that the modern state and the idea of a countable population are historical co-productions, premised alike on distinctively modern constructions of governance, territory, and citizenship. Censuses are salient among the techniques identified by Foucault (1979) as lying at the heart of modern governmentality. Tied up by their nature with the state (note the etymological link with statistics) and its methods of classification and surveillance, censuses remain essential instruments of every modern state archive. They are highly politicized processes, whose results are usually available only in packaged form and whose procedures are always driven from above, even when many members of the population are enlisted in the actual gathering of data. Given this background, it seems all the more remarkable that, without adherence to any articulated theory of governmentality – or opposition to it – the Alliance has adopted a conscious strategy of self-enumeration and self-surveying. Alliance members are taught a variety of methods of gathering reliable and complete data about households and families in

their own communities. Codifying these techniques for ease of use by its members in the form of a series of practical tips, the Alliance has created a revolutionary system that we may well call governmentality from below.

Not only has it placed self-surveying at the heart of its own archive, the Alliance is also keenly aware of the power that this kind of knowledge – and ability – gives it in its dealings with local and central state organizations (as well as with multilateral agencies and other regulatory bodies). The leverage bestowed by such information is particularly acute in places like Mumbai, where a host of local, state-level, and federal entities exist with a mandate to rehabilitate or ameliorate slum life. But none of them knows exactly who the slum dwellers are, where they live, or how they are to be identified. This fact is of central relevance to the politics of knowledge in which the Alliance is perennially engaged. All state-sponsored slum policies have an abstract slum population as their target and no knowledge of its concrete, human components. Since these populations are socially, legally, and spatially marginal – invisible citizens, as it were – they are by definition uncounted and uncountable, except in the most general terms.

By rendering them statistically visible to themselves, the Alliance comes into control of a central piece of any actual policy process – the knowledge of exactly which individuals live where, how they make their livelihood, how long they have lived there, and so forth. Given that some of the most crucial pieces of recent legislation affecting slum dwellers in Mumbai tie security of tenure to the date from which occupancy of a piece of land or a structure can be demonstrated, such information collection is vital to any official effort to relocate and rehabilitate slum populations.

At the same time, the creation and use of self-surveys are a powerful tool for the practice of democracy internally, since the principal form of evidence used by the Alliance to support slum dwellers' claims to space is the testimony of neighbors, as opposed to forms of documentation such as rent receipts, ration cards, electric meter readings, and other civic insignia of occupancy that can be used by the more securely housed classes in the city. The very absence of these amenities opens the door to radical techniques of mutual identification in the matter of location and legitimacy for slum dwellers. For, as Alliance leaders are the first to admit, the poor are not immune to greed, conflict, and jealousy, and there are always slum families who are prepared to lie or cheat to advance themselves in the context of crisis or new opportunities. Such problems are resolved by informal mechanisms in which the testimony of neighbors is utterly decisive, since the social life of slums is in fact characterized by an almost complete lack of privacy. Here, perpetual social visibility within the community (and invisibility in the eyes of the state) becomes an asset that enables the mechanisms of self-monitoring, self-enumerating, and self-regulation to operate at the nexus of family, land, and dwelling that is the central site of material negotiations in slum life.

To those familiar with Foucault's ideas, this may seem to be a worrisome form of autogovernmentality, a combination of self-surveillance and self-enumeration, truly insidious in its capillary reach. But my own view is that this sort of govern-mentality from below, in the world of the urban poor, is a kind of countergovernmentality, animated by the social relations of shared poverty, by the excitement of active participation in the politics of knowledge, and by its own openness to correction through other forms of intimate knowledge and spontaneous everyday politics. In short, this is governmentality turned against itself.

Housing exhibitions are the second organized technique through which the structural bias of existing knowledge processes is challenged, even reversed, in the politics of the Alliance. Since the materialities of housing – its cost, its durability, its legality, and its design – are of fundamental concern to slum life, it is no surprise that this is an area where grassroots creativity has had radical effects. As in other matters, the general philosophy of state agencies, donors, and even NGOs concerned with slums has been to assume that the design, construction, and financing of houses require the involvement of various experts and knowledge professionals, ranging from engineers and architects to contractors and surveyors. The Alliance has challenged this assumption by a steady effort to appropriate, in a cumulative manner, all the knowledge required to construct new housing for its members. This has involved some extraordinary negotiations in Mumbai, involving private developers and contractors, the formation of legal cooperatives by the poor, innovations in urban law pushed by the Alliance, new types of arrangements in housing finance between banks, donors, and the poor themselves, and direct negotiations over housing materials, costs, and building schedules. In effect, in

Mumbai, the Alliance has moved into housing development, and the fruits of this remarkable move are to be seen at three major sites, in Mankhurd, Dharavi, and Ghatkopar. One of these, the Rajiv-Indira Housing Cooperative in Dharavi, is a major building exercise that stands as a decisive demonstration of the Alliance's ability to put the actual families who will occupy these dwellings at the center of a process where credit, design, budgeting, construction, and legality come together. It is difficult to exaggerate the complexity of such negotiations, which pose a challenge even for wealthy developers because of the maze of laws, agencies, and political interests (including those of the criminal underworld) that surrounds any housing enterprise in Mumbai.

Housing exhibitions are a crucial part of this reversal of the standard flows of expert knowledge. The idea of housing exhibitions by and for the poor goes back to 1986 in Mumbai and has since been replicated in many other cities in India and elsewhere in the world. The exhibitions organized by the Alliance and other like-minded groups are an example of the creative hijacking of an upper-class form – historically developed for the display of consumer goods and high-end industrial products – for the purposes of the poor.

Not only have these exhibitions enabled the poor, especially poor women, to discuss and debate designs for housing that suit their own needs, they have also allowed the poor to enter into conversations with various professionals about housing materials, construction costs, and urban services. Through this process, slum dwellers' own ideas of the good life, of adequate space, and of realistic costs were foregrounded, and they began to see that professional housing construction was only a logical extension of their own area of greatest expertise – namely, building adequate housing out of the flimsiest of materials and in the most insecure of circumstances. Poor families were enabled to see that they had always been architects and engineers and could continue to play these roles in the building of more secure housing. In this process, many technical and design innovations were made, and continue to be made. Perhaps more significantly, the exhibitions have been political events bringing together poor families and activists from different cities in order to socialize, share ideas, and simply have fun. State officials also are invited, to cut the ceremonial ribbon and give speeches in which they associate themselves with these grassroots exercises, thus simultaneously gaining points for hobnobbing with "the people" while giving poor families in the locality some legitimacy in the eyes of their neighbors, civic authorities, and themselves.

As with other key practices of the Alliance, housing exhibitions are deep exercises in subverting the existing class cultures of India. By performing their competencies in public, by addressing an audience of their peers and of representatives of the state, other NGOs, and sometimes foreign funders, the poor families involved enter a space of public sociality, official recognition, and technical legitimation. And they do so with their own creativity as the main exhibit. Thus technical and cultural capital are generated collaboratively by these events, creating leverage for further guerrilla exercises in capturing civic space and areas of the public sphere hitherto denied them. At work here is a politics of visibility that inverts the harmful default condition of civic invisibility that characterizes the urban poor.

Running through all these activities is a spirit of transgression and bawdiness expressed through body language, speech styles, and public address. The men and women of the Alliance are involved in constant banter with one another and even with the official world (although with some care for context). Nowhere is this carnivalesque spirit displayed more clearly than in the toilet festivals (sandas mela) organized by the Alliance, which enact what we may call the politics of shit.

Human waste management, as it is euphemistically termed in policy circles, is perhaps the key issue where every problem of the urban poor arrives at a single point of extrusion, so to speak. Given the abysmal housing, often with almost no privacy, that most urban slum dwellers endure, shitting in public is a serious humiliation for adults. Children are indifferent up to a certain age, but no adult, male or female, enjoys shitting in broad daylight in public view. In rural India, women go to the fields to defecate while it is still dark; men may go later, but nevertheless with some measure of protection from the eyes of the public (with the exception of the railway passengers, inured to the sight of the squatting bodies in the fields, whose attitude is reciprocated). But the fact is that rural shitting is managed through a completely different economy of space, water, visibility, and custom from that prevailing in cities, where the problem is much more serious.

Shitting in the absence of good sewerage systems, ventilation, and running water – all of which, by definition, slums lack – is not only humiliating, it also enables the conditions under which waterborne diseases take hold and thus is potentially life-threatening. One macabre joke among Mumbai's urban poor is that they are the only ones in the city who cannot afford to get diarrhea. Lines at the few existing public toilets are often so long that the wait is an hour or more, and of course medical facilities for stemming the condition are also hard to find. In short, shitting and its management are a central issue of slum life. Living in an ecology of fecal odors, piles, and channels, where cooking water, washing water, and shit-bearing water are not carefully segregated, adds material health risks to the symbolic risks incurred by shitting in public view.

The toilet festivals organized by the Alliance in many cities of India are a brilliant effort to resituate this private act of humiliation and suffering as the scene of technical innovation, collective celebration, and carnivalesque play with officials from the state, the World Bank, and middle-class officialdom in general. The toilet festivals feature the exhibition and inauguration not of models, but of functioning public toilets designed by and for the poor, incorporating complex systems of collective payment and maintenance with optimal conditions of safety and cleanliness. These facilities are currently small scale and have not yet been built in anything like the large numbers required for India's slum populations. But they represent another performance of competence and innovation in which the politics of shit is (to mix metaphors) turned on its head, and humiliation and victimization are transformed into exercises in technical initiative and self-dignification.

This is nothing less than a politics of recognition (Taylor 1992) from below. When a World Bank official has to examine the virtues of a public toilet and discuss the merits of this form of shit management with the shitters themselves, the condition of poverty moves from abjection to subjectivation. The politics of shit – as Gandhi showed in his own efforts to liberate the lowest castes, whom he called Harijans, from the task of hauling upper-caste ordure – presents a node at which concerns of the human body, dignity, and technology meet, a nexus the poor are now redefining with the help of movements like the Alliance. In India, where distance from one's own excrement can be seen as the virtual marker of class distinction, the poor, for too long having lived literally in their own shit, are finding ways to place some distance between their waste and themselves. The toilet exhibitions are a transgressive display of this fecal politics, itself a critical material feature of deep democracy.

In June 2001, at a major meeting held at the United Nations to mark the five years that had passed since the 1996 Conference on Human Settlements in Istanbul, the Alliance and its international partners built a model house as well as a model children's toilet in the lobby of the main UN building. The models – which were erected only after considerable internal debate within the Shack/Slum Dwellers International (SDI) and official resistance at the UN – were visited by Secretary-General Kofi Annan in a festive atmosphere that left an indelible impression on the officials of the UN and other NGOs who were present. Annan was surrounded by poor women from India and South Africa who sang and danced as he walked through the model house and toilet that had been placed in the heart of his own bureaucratic empire. It was a magical moment, full of possibilities for the Alliance, and for the secretary-general, as they engage jointly with the politics of global poverty. Housing exhibitions and toilets, too, can be built, moved, refabricated, and deployed anywhere, thus sending the message that no space is too grand – or too humble – for the spatial imagination of the poor.

These organized practices sustain one another. Self-surveys form the basis of claims to new housing and justify its exhibition; model housing built without due attention to toilets and fecal management makes no sense. Each of these methods uses the knowledge of the poor to leverage expert knowledge, redeems humiliation through a politics of recognition, and enables the deepening of democracy among the poor themselves. And each of them adds energy and purpose to the others. They enact public dramas in which the moral directives to federate, to save, and to set precedents are made material, refined, and revalidated. In this way, key words and deeds shape one another, permitting some leveling of the field of knowledge, turning sites of shame into dramas of inclusion, and allowing the poor to work their way into the public sphere and visible citizenship without resort to open confrontation or public violence.

THE INTERNATIONAL HORIZON

The larger study of which this essay is a part is concerned with the way in which transnational advocacy networks, associations of grassroots NGOs, are in the process of internationalizing themselves, thus creating networks of globalization from below. We have seen such networks mobilized most recently in Seattle, Prague, Göteborg, and Washington, D.C. But they have been visible for some time in global struggles over gender issues, the environment, human rights, child labor, and the rights of indigenous cultures. More recently, there has been a

renewed effort to link grassroots activists in such diverse areas as violence against women, the rights of refugees and immigrants, the employment of sweatshop labor by multinational corporations, indigenous peoples' claims to intellectual property, the production and consumption of popular media, mediation between combatants in civil conflicts, and many other issues. The underlying question for many of these movements is: How can they organize transnationally without sacrificing their local projects? When they do build transnational networks, what are their greatest assets and their greatest handicaps? At a deeper political level, can the mobility of capital and new information technologies be contained by, and made accountable to, the ethos and purpose of local democratic projects? Put another way, can there be a new design for global governance that mediates the speed of capital, the power of states, and the profoundly local nature of actually existing democracies?

These large questions go beyond the scope of this essay, and the detailed analysis of the efforts to globalize from below of this activist network, and others like it, must be left for another occasion. But a brief account of this global context is certainly in order. For more than a decade the Alliance in Mumbai has been an active part of a transnational network concerned with "horizontal learning," sharing, and exchanging. Given official form as the Shack/Slum Dwellers International, or SDI, in 1996, the network includes federations in fourteen countries on four continents. The process that led to this formalization goes back to the mid-1980s. Links among federations of the poor in South Africa, India, and Thailand appear to have been the most vital in the gradual building of these grassroots exchanges and, to a considerable extent, still are. Key to these exchanges are visits by groups of slum or shack dwellers to one another's settlements in other countries to share in ongoing local projects, give and receive advice and reactions, share in work and life experiences, and exchange tactics and plans. The mode of exchange is based on a model of seeing and hearing rather than of teaching and learning; of sharing experiences and knowledge rather than seeking to impose standard practices, key words being exposure, exploration, and options. By now, a large body of practical wisdom has accrued about how and when these exchanges work best, and this knowledge is constantly being refined. Visits by small groups from one city to another, either within the same or to another region, usually involve immediate immersion in the ongoing projects of the host community. These range from scavenging in the Philippines and sewer digging in Pakistan to women's savings activities in South Africa and housing exhibitions in India.

These horizontal exchanges now function at four levels. First, they provide a circulatory counterpart to the building of deep democracies locally. By visiting and hosting other activists concerned with similar problems, communities gain a comparative perspective and provide a measure of legitimation for external efforts. Thus, activist leaders struggling for recognition and space in their own localities may find themselves able to gain state and media attention for their local struggles in other countries and towns, where their presence as visitors carries a certain cachet. The fact that they are visiting as members of some sort of international federation further sharpens this image. In fact, local politicians feel less threatened by visitors than by their own activists and sometimes open themselves to new ideas because they come from outside.

Second, the horizontal visits arranged by the federations increasingly carry the imprimatur of powerful international organizations and funders such as the World Bank, state development ministries, and private charities from the Netherlands, England, the United States, and Germany, and increasingly involve political and philanthropic actors from other countries as well. These visits, designed and organized by the poor in their own communities and public spaces, become signs to local politicians that the poor themselves have cosmopolitan links – a factor that increases their prestige in local political negotiations.

Third, the occasions that these exchanges provide for face-to-face meetings between key leaders in, for example, Mumbai, Cape Town, and Bangkok actually allow them to progress rapidly in making more long-term strategic plans for funding, capacity building, and what they call scaling up, which is now perhaps their central aim. That is, having mastered how to do certain things on a small scale, they are eager to expand onto a broader canvas, seeking collective ways of making a dent in the vast range of problems shared by slum dwellers in different cities. In a parallel movement, they are also exploring ways of speeding up, by which they mean shortening the times involved in putting strategies into practice in different national and urban locations.

There is some evidence that speeding up through horizontal learning is somewhat easier than scaling up. In support of the latter goal, the core SDI leadership is working on ways to build a transnational funding mechanism that will reduce the federations' dependence on existing multilateral and private sources, putting even long-term funding in the hands of the SDI so as to free its members further from the agendas of project planners, donors, states, and other actors, whose aims can never be quite the same as those of the urban poor. Elements of such a mechanism exist among the South African and Thai members of the SDI, but the structure is yet to be realized on a fully global scale. That will require the current leadership of SDI to proceed with a demanding mixture of political cooperation, willingness to negotiate, and stubbornness of vision in their dialogues with the major funders of the battle against urban poverty worldwide. The objective of creating a worldwide fund controlled by a pro-poor activist network is the logical extension of a politics of patience combined with a politics of visibility and self-empowerment. It is directly pitched against the politics of charity, training, and projectization long recognized as the standard solution. As such, it represents a formidable wager on the capacities of the poor to create large-scale, high-speed, reliable mechanisms for the change of conditions that affect them globally. The proposal for a coordinated funding mechanism inaugurates a new vision for equalizing material resources and knowledge at one stroke. The self-organization of this network is very much in process and constitutes an ongoing experiment in globalization from below and in deep democracy.

The fourth, and most important, level at which the traffic

among local and national units functions within the Shack/ Slum Dwellers International is that of the circulation of internal critical debate. When members of the SDI meet in one another's localities (as well as on other occasions, such as meetings in London, New York, or the Hague), they have the occasion to raise hard questions about inclusion, power, hierarchy, and political risk or naïveté in their host's local and regional organizations. This is because their role as outsiders allows for frank questions, based on real or rhetorical ignorance – questions that would frequently be regarded as unacceptable coming from closer quarters.

Who handles the money? Why are there not more women at the meeting? Why are you being so nice to the city officials who oppress you? How do you deal with defaulters on small loans? Who is doing the real work? Who is getting the perks of foreign travel? Why are we staying in one kind of hotel and you in another? Why are some poor people in your city for you and others against you? Why did your savings group start falling apart? Are you happy with this or that leader? Is someone getting too big for his boots? Are we beginning to take up partnerships that might fail us in the long run? When we agree to a global agenda, which national partner is really setting it? How far should we go in trusting each other's intuitions about partners, strategies, and priorities?

These are some of the tough questions that are asked by friendly but skeptical visitors, and usually answered frankly by the local hosts. And when the answers are weak or unsatisfying, they continue to reverberate in the locality, long after the visitors have returned to their home communities. This critical exchange is a long-term asset, a vital part of globalization from below. The visits – and the e-mails that sustain the interims – incorporate a crucial dimension through which the challenge of facing internal criticism can be mediated: distance. The global network of poor communities turns out to be, among other things, a constant source of critical questions about theory and practice, a flow of irritating queries, doubts, and pauses. But coming from a distance, they sound less harsh than the same queries when they come from local opponents. At the same time, coming from communities equally poor, their moral urgency cannot be ignored.

It is this last consideration that now allows us to return to the relations among risk, creativity, and depth in the democratic experiments of the Alliance and its global network, the SDI. The Alliance and the transnational network of which it is a part belong to a group of nongovernmental actors that have decided to opt for various sorts of partnerships with other, more powerful actors – including the state, in its various levels and incarnations – to achieve its goals: to gain secure housing and urban infrastructure for the urban poor, in Mumbai, in other parts of India, and beyond. In opting for the politics of partnership, such movements consciously undertake certain risks. One is the risk that their partners may not hold even some moral goals in common with them. Another is that the hard-won mobilization of certain groups of the urban poor may not be best invested as political capital in partnership arrangements, as opposed to confrontation or violence.

And there is an even larger gamble involved in this strategy. This is the gamble that the official world of multilateral agencies, Northern funders, and Southern governments can be persuaded that the poor are the best drivers of shared solutions to the problems of poverty. What is at stake here is all the energy that has been invested in setting precedents for partnership at all levels, from the ward to the world. The hoped-for payoff is that, once mobilized and empowered by such partnerships, the poor themselves will prove more capable than the usual candidates – the market, the state, or the world of development funding – of scaling up and speeding up their own disappearance as a global category. In the end, this is a political wager on the relationship between the circulation of knowledge and material equalization, and about the best ways to accelerate it.

In making this wager, activist groups like the Alliance in Mumbai and its global counterparts are also striving to redefine what governance and govern-mentality can mean. They approach their partners on an ad hoc basis, taking advantage in particular of the dispersed nature of the state as an apparatus of local, regional, and national bodies to advance their long-term aims and form multilateral relationships. Moreover, in a country like India, where poverty reduction is a directive principle of the national constitution and the tradition of social reform and public service is woven into nationalism itself, the Alliance can play the politics of conscience to considerable effect. But even then, it hedges its

bets through practices of building on, sharing, and multiplying knowledge – strategic practices that increase its hold on public resources.

CONCLUSION: DEEP DEMOCRACY

One of the many paradoxes of democracy is that it is organized to function within the boundaries of the nation-state – through such organs as legislatures, judiciaries, and elected governments – to realize one or another image of the common good or general will. Yet its values make sense only when they are conceived and deployed universally, which is to say, when they are global in reach. Thus, the institutions of democracy and its cardinal values rest on an antinomy. In the era of globalization, this contradiction rises to the surface as the porousness of national boundaries becomes apparent and the monopoly of national governments over global governance becomes increasingly embattled.

Efforts to enact or revive democratic principles have generally taken two forms in the period since 1970, which many agree is the beginning of globalization (or of the current era of globalization, for those who wish to write globalization into the whole of human history). One form is to take advantage of the speed of communications and the sweep of global markets to force national governments to recognize universal democratic principles within their own jurisdictions. Much of the politics of human rights takes this form. The second form, more fluid and quixotic, is the sort that I have described here. It constitutes an effort to institute what we may call "democracy without borders," after the analogy of international class solidarity as conceived by the visionaries of world socialism in its heyday. This effort is what I seek to theorize in terms of deep democracy.

In terms of its semantics, deep democracy suggests roots, anchors, intimacy, proximity, and locality. And these are important associations. Much of this essay has been taken up with values and strategies that have just this quality. They are about such traditional democratic desiderata as inclusion, participation, transparency, and accountability, as articulated within an activist formation. But I want to suggest that the lateral reach of such movements – their efforts to build international networks or coalitions of some durability with their counterparts across national boundaries – is also a part of their "depth."

This lateral or horizontal dimension, which I have touched upon in terms of the activities of the Shack/Slum Dwellers International, seeks direct collaborations and exchanges among poor communities based on the "will to federate." But what gives this cross-national politics its depth is not just its circulatory logic of spreading ideas of savings, housing, citizenship, and participation "without borders" and outside the direct reach of state or market regimes. Depth is also to be located in the fact that, where successful, the spread of this model produces poor communities able to engage in partnerships with more powerful agencies – urban, regional, national, and multilateral – that purport to be concerned with poverty and citizenship. In this second sense, what these horizontal movements produce is a series of stronger community-based partners for institutional agencies charged with realizing inclusive democracy and poverty reduction. This in turn increases the capability of these communities to perform more powerfully as instruments of deep democracy in the local context. The cycles of transactions – both vertical (local/national) and horizontal (transnational/global) – are enriched by the process of criticism by members of one federated community, in the context of exchange and learning, about the internal democracy of another. Thus, internal criticism and debate, horizontal exchange and learning, and vertical collaborations and partnerships with more powerful persons and organizations together form a mutually sustaining cycle of processes. This is where depth and laterality become joint circuits along which pro-poor strategies can flow.

This form of deep democracy, the vertical fulcrum of a democracy without borders, cannot be assumed to be automatic, easy, or immune to setbacks. Like all serious exercises in democratic practice, it is not automatically reproductive. It has particular conditions of possibility and conditions under which it grows weak or corrupt. The study of these conditions – which include such contingencies as leadership, morale, flexibility, and material enablement – requires many more case studies of specific movements and organizations. For those concerned with poverty and citizenship, we can begin by recalling that one crucial condition of possibility for deep democracy is the ability to meet emergency with patience.

ARJUN APPADURAI

6:2

Arjun Appadurai is Samuel N. Harper Distinguished Service Professor of Anthropology and South Asian Languages and Civilizations at the University of Chicago. His recent publications include "Grassroots Globalization and the Research Imagination" (Public Culture, winter 2000) and "New Logics of Violence" (Seminar, July 2001).

This essay is based on research funded by the Ford Foundation. I owe special thanks to Carol A. Breckenridge, who first suggested to me that the work of the Mumbai Alliance could be characterized in the image of "deep democracy." The first draft of this essay was written in June 2000 at the University of Amsterdam's School of Social Science Research, where I was honored to serve as a Distinguished Visiting Professor. Since then, it has been debated by audiences in Chicago, Buenos Aires, Montevideo, and Paris. For their useful criticism and help in organizing these discussions, I must thank Marc Abélès, Hugo Achugar, Irene Belier, Partha Chatterjee, Dilip Parameshwar Gaonkar, Christophe Jaffrelot, Elizabeth Jelin, Benjamin Lee, Achille Mbembe, Mariella Pandolfi, Charles Taylor, and Peter van der Veer. In a separate vein, I owe thanks to various members and supporters of the Alliance in India and the Shack/Slum Dwellers International network for their critical support and encouragement of the research process and the direction of the first draft: to Arputham Jockin, Srilatha Batliwala, Somsook Boonyabancha, William Cobbett, Celine d'Cruz, Ellen Schaengold, Marjolijn Wilmink, and Patrick Wakely, in addition to Joel Bolnick, Sundar Burra, Diana Mitlin, Ruth McLeod, and Sheela Patel, whose own draft papers have helped me to get a more balanced picture of the Alliance's activities. This essay also appears in Environment and Urbanization 13 (2002).

REFERENCES

Appadurai, Arjun. 1996. Modernity at large: Cultural dimensions of globalization. Minneapolis: University of Minnesota Press.
———. 2000. Grassroots globalization and the research imagination. Public Culture 12: 1–19.
———. 2001. Spectral housing and urban cleansing: Notes on millennial Mumbai. Public Culture 12: 627–51.
Appadurai, Arjun, and Holston, James. 1999. Introduction: Cities and citizenship. In Cities and citizenship, edited by Holston. Durham, N.C.: Duke University Press.
Bindé, Jérôme. 2000. Toward an ethics of the future. Public Culture 12: 51–72.
Castells, Manuel. 1996. The rise of the network society. Cambridge, Mass.: Blackwell.
Foucault, Michel. 1979. Governmentality. In The Foucault effect: Studies in governmentality: With two lectures by and an interview with Michel Foucault, edited by Graham Burchell, Colin Gordon, and Peter Miller. Chicago: University of Chicago Press.
Giddens, Anthony. 2000. Runaway world: How globalization is reshaping our lives. New York: Routledge.
Habermas, Jürgen. 1975. Legitimation crisis, translated by Thomas McCarthy. Boston: Beacon.
Held, David. 1995. Democracy and the global order: From the modern state to cosmopolitan governance. Stanford, Calif.: Stanford University Press.
Keck, Margaret E., and Kathryn Sikkink. 1998. Activists beyond borders: Advocacy networks in international politics. Ithaca, N.Y.: Cornell University Press.
Pendse, Sandeep. 1995. Toil, sweat and the city. In Bombay: Metaphor for modern India, edited by Sujata Patel and Alice Thorner. Bombay: Oxford University Press.
Rosenau, James N. 1997. Along the domestic-foreign frontier: Exploring governance in a turbulent world. Cambridge: Cambridge University Press.
Sassen, Saskia. 2000. Spatialities and temporalities of the global: Elements for a theorization. Public Culture 12: 215–32.
Taylor, Charles. 1992. The politics of recognition. In Multiculturalism and "The politics of recognition," edited by Amy Gutmann and Charles Taylor. Princeton, N.J.: Princeton University Press.

6:3

6:3   Jockin with a map of Dharavi, attempting to explain the consequences of the masterplan.

MR JOCKIN — AN INTERNATIONAL LEADER

Jockin Arputham has lived in Dharavi for over 40 years. He is one of the founders and the director of the organization Slum Dwellers International (SDI), a movement dedicated to the mobilization and empowerment of squatters. SDI has spread to 23 countries around the world. Jockin is also one of the founding members of SPARC, the Society for the Promotion of Area Resource Centres.

According to Jockin, one of the most effective ways to empower the poor is to use shared savings. Organizations that pool their contributions, such as Mahila Milan, give their participants the scope to develop solutions within their own communities.

"The poorest of the poor are being marginalized all the time. They are not getting their space because the planners have ignored them. In Mumbai 55 to 65 percent of people are living in slums in unsuitable conditions. If their voices are not heard locally or globally, their number will only increase … In order to make society at large hear them, we need to tell the world that we are finding solutions to our own problems. The solution will not come from others. What we need is for people to listen to what our community has to say. We are not begging or asking for total charity, we need to be participants. We need to be part of the development of our own people. We can not sit and wait for somebody to come and feed us."

The urban poor can and should come together collectively, Jockin says, and they are definitely getting organized on a global scale.

"Yes, we have organized ourselves. We are not waiting for the government or the donors to deliver. We are tired of waiting and watching and waiting."

JHE

MAHILA MILAN

Mahila Milan is Hindi for "Women Together" and can be described as a de-centralised network consisting of poor women who, among other things, organize credit and savings in their local area.

Mahila Milan started in 1986 when some 500 women living on the pavements of Mumbai started to organize themselves in order to stall evictions and to stop the demolition of their homes that were taking space every fortnight. Many of these women became friends and started to discuss what to do next. Today Mahila Milan has given tens of thousands of loans to women all over India and has accumulated common savings worth tens of millions of rupees.

One of the areas that the women pinpointed was the need for reliable loans that could help with day-to-day crises. Since they had no, or very little money, they had to either borrow from each other or else fall into the hands of loan sharks. Mahila Milan solved this problem by creating a collective self-help system.

Mahila Milan's set-up process was very simple: every stretch of pavement on a street in Mumbai normally holds between 10 and 15 households; one woman from each "street group" was elected to make daily visits to all the households on her street and take care of the deposits, loans and repayments. All of these transactions are carefully noted in two books, one personal notebook and one general control-book for the whole group.

In the beginning, Mahila Milan used different pieces of coloured paper to represent the amounts of loans and savings since many of the women are illiterate. Today they leave big blue fingerprints as signatures in the books. Members of Mahila Milan save for both short term economic problems and longer term housing plans.

Each of the women representatives also participates in a committee that takes decisions about the payment of loans. Each committee has its own rules for loans and repayment, but a prevailing factor is that the loans can be given out at any time of the day or night, since it is the women in the local neighbourhood who make the administrative decisions.

It might seem odd and even unnecessarily bureaucratic to save such small amounts every single day instead of just depositing larger sums on a regular bases, but this system is one of the strengths of Mahila Milan. If these women were asked to save 30 rupees each month, they would perceive it as a very difficult thing to do. The handling of larger sums of money can cause problems. But, as one woman from the collective stated, "If I am to save 1 rupee per day then, for example, my son agrees to skip his daily sweet and we will hardly notice that we are saving. At the end of the month 30 rupees are saved without any major effort at all. Earlier, we did not know how to save money, if we had some change it would just disappear."

Mahila Milan started off on a few pavements in Byculla, Mumbai and has now spread across the city and to many other places in India. Even if the individual amounts are small, the benefits of this organization go beyond the basic needs they help sustain. Indeed, these women learn from their experience with Mahila Milan to handle transactions and negotiate in many other aspects of life. Mahila Milan has created a visible impact to people's immediate environment. This has helped the women involved become more respected in their communities and other financial institutions are also taking Mahila Milan seriously. Banks, for instance, use the Mahila Milan's written documentation concerning old loan repayments when assessing women's applications for larger loans.

Whilst women are often the ones who bare the brunt of social deprivation in India, it is also the case that they are excluded from much of the decision making in family and political life. Mahila Milan has succeeded in including women in every stage of its development. By building their initiatives from "within", the women of Mahila Milan have created strategies for the social and economic problems closest at hand; they have built solutions which will remain flexible as each empowered woman's individual set of circumstances continues to change and grow.

JHE / SE

6:4

6:4 Preema Salgoonkan in the pink dress is always moving. She has a lot of responsibilities when she oversees the Mahila Milan accounts and she also fills an important social role.

6:5 Mahila Milan savings book. Every transaction is carefully noted.

6:6 Preema counting the savings at the end of the day before closing the books.

6:7 This elderly man is sitting in his cramped "hole-in-the-wall" sorting someone else's waste that he has bought and will re-sell later. With the help of Mahila Milan he is saving money for a decent funeral when the time comes. He puts aside a few coins every day. Since he no longer has any relatives, he has given Preema from Mahila Milan detailed instructions on how his funeral is to be conducted.

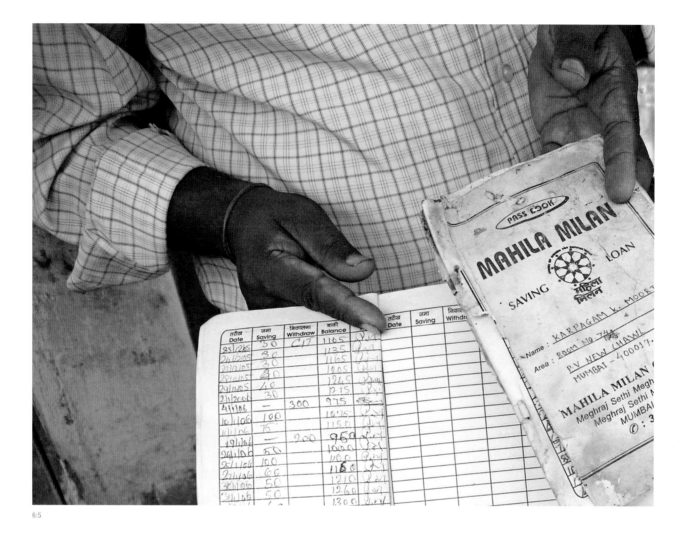

6:5

6:6

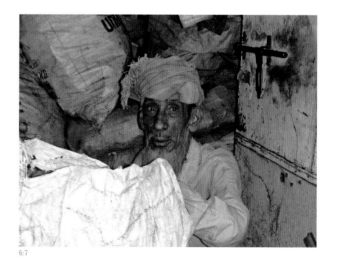

6:7

Collecting Savings

PREEMA SALGOONKAN

Indu is frying chapatis on a small open fire. She has collected the sticks. Two children can be spotted at the far end of her home. Indu is pleased to proudly present a ten-rupee note to Preema. This is what she is able to save today. She is mainly saving so that she can rent a room for the family (along with two other families) during the monsoon season when this stretch of land by the busy railway tracks will be even less liveable than it already is.

Preema (in the red dress) has worked for seventeen years collecting money. She tells me that the women in Dharavi have divided the area into several districts. Preema has 400-800 households in her district. She complains that her feet ache nowadays. She covers several miles every morning when she collects savings.

Preema is a widow. Her spouse died only three years after they wed. She has two children, a son and a daughter.

In the afternoon, after she has counted and deposited all the worn paper bills at the Mahila Milan office, she takes a sort break with a crossword or a Sudoku-like puzzle. Preema likes numbers and is quick at mental arithmetic.

Valli and Pachiamma are also savings collectors, and they are meticulous when they write down numbers in their books.

In the afternoon a small stream of women come into the office to pick up their loans. Most of them do not sign their names because they are illiterate, instead they press their thumbs against the ink pad and then carefully leave a mark in the books.

Preema has worked for Mahila Milan for almost two decades and there has been a lot of changes.

"Yes, yes." Preema says, "Today so many people are working and the standard of living is increasing. We give them loans and they start their own businesses. The ladies have small, small businesses. Before Mahila Milan started only the men were working and giving small amounts of money to their wives. Today women are very confident. Each and every woman has to work, they are out of the house and doing work, so they are earning a little bit more. Mainly they run small-scale businesses, only one or two women together, no large-scale business. Everybody who saves is able to start a business of her own. Let's say someone saved 1000 rupees and wants a loan – she will get the loan if she has a good plan for the money.

"Today there is a national level project, Rashtria Mahila Cause, The National Women's Fund. The government secures lots of money for the development of women. It is a loan for new businesses. It started in 1992 and SPARC had a great role in this."

Preema walks around her district every day, "I arrive at nine in the morning and I go home at seven". She works her ten hours even on Saturdays and Sundays, but not only collecting money.

"I also help with family matters." she says. "There are domestic problems, school problems and there are always economic problems. Sometimes even problems that end up at the hospital. Like recently when my neighbour came knocking on my door at two o'clock in the night yelling – Preema, Preema, my son has drunk poison! Of course I had to go with them to the hospital even if it was in the middle of the night."

6:8   Preema collecting savings by the railway.

"Or there was another problem, one woman comes crying – my husband beat me – so I try to solve their problem. Or problems with school's admission fees."

Preema argues that the real matters essentially are the family matters, "Husband and wife. Small quarrels that occur in the house and we are dealing with them, but the very big things no ... You know, most of the people here have a really low living standard and some of them are always searching for money. Like if this guy has stolen something from that shop, these kinds of matters are handled by the police, not by us".

"The poverty is the main problem – of course housing and shelter also – but in Dharavi so many people have so much money and some people have no money at all. Yes, there is a very nasty big difference. Many, many rich people here, like smugglers, working at night ... but most people, normal people, they are below the poverty line."

I ask her how to solve such a problem, how to solve the poverty? If there is any political will to do anything about it. Preema laughs, "Politicians do not care, they only come for their work and nothing else. They only come here when there is an election coming up, otherwise no ... But the SPARC people do, and the Mahila Milan, the savings are one part and creating jobs is another part. Personal engagement and creating jobs will make a proper slum."

SE

INDU

Indu is a second-generation beggar. She works inside the trains together with her children, just as her parents did when Indu was a child.

The family (2007) consists of: The husband Nala (35) and Indu (30). Their sons Subhas (13) and Arjun (7). Their daughters, Arti (3) and her sister (1).

Indu has given birth to six children. The children were all born at home, without any assistance, two of them died at 18 and 2 months of age.

Indu says, "There is a private clinic which charges 50 rupees for an adult and 20 rupees for a child per visit. Medicine costs between 100 and 200 rupees."

Sarkari Hospital is the name of the municipal hospital, which is cheaper.

"But I am afraid" Indu says, "I don't want to go there. They take out your blood and they steal organs." She tells us the appalling story of one person who 'got rid of' his kidney. Indu prefers the private clinic.

"If you go to the hospital you have to sit and wait the whole day and you loose your income that day." But earlier, when Indu had tuberculosis, she went to Sarkari hospital and was prescribed medicine for three months. After this she got well again. Now, with a beautiful smile, she says she's fine.

The children do not have any birth certificates. This is because it costs 200 rupees and Indu and Nala cannot fill out the necessary forms because they are illiterate.

Indu was born near the Banda-Kurla Complex. Between four and five families were living in that area, but building work forced them to relocate. They were four children and Indu was very small when she started to beg with her mother on the trains. Indu sees begging as a job – some people give you money and some don't.

"But white people seem to have a better situation." she says.

She was 18 years old when she married Nala. Nala used to live in a village near Kolapur, Maharastra, before coming to Mumbai. Nowadays he works at weddings and sells garlands at traffic lights. He has started to smoke a lot of cannabis, possibly due to his meagre situation.

"There is nobody to support us. I cannot ask for a loan, so I go begging." Indu says, "I can earn between 30 and 40 rupees a day and I eat the leftovers from the neighbourhood. My husband can earn a maximum of 140 rupees a day."

Indu does not have a ration card with which the poorest can acquire rice, lentils and so on at subsidised rates in government stores. To receive a ration card you must prove that you have a permanent address, but since their home is considered temporary and is in an illegal tent camp on the railroad's territory, Indu will never get a permanent address. Indu's only chance to get a ration card is to bribe a civil servant so that she can get a false address.

"But that would cost me 6000 rupees." she says, "And where will I get that much money?"

During the heavy rainstorms and floods of the monsoon season they must move around. Sometimes up on the railway platform and sometimes to her mother's place in Mankurd.

"But it becomes too crowded there, two brothers, two wives plus all the children and the parents." Indu says.

"Nobody is with us to guide us how to bring up children and I have no aspirations at all." No dreams of a better future. When asked about her view on school for her children, she replies, "No, they would only run back home, it is no good. And the teachers beat them. If I have money I will get my children married, otherwise …"

Indu stopped saving four months ago. She took all the money she had saved, 300 rupees, closed her Mahila Milan account and went to the Gods festival in Pune.

"My next life only depends on God." she says.

SE

6:9

6:9   Indu's home.

6:10   Indu with two of her children.

6:10

NASEEMA BANU

6:11

Naseema Banu was just a girl when she came to Mumbai from Uttar Pradesh in northern India. Now she has children of her own and wants to inspire them to work for themselves. She hopes to do this by showing them the results of her own hard work. Naseema has six children aged 6, 10, 12, 16, 19 and 20. One is a carpenter who wants to work, but not study. One of her daughters loves to study and dreams of becoming a doctor.

They live in a good area. All the neighbours have been saving money with Mahila Milan for the last seven years. Originally the family lived on the pipeline without a place of their own, but now they have built a one-room house with a kitchenette. In the image we can see that the house is partially constructed with corrugated iron. The kitchen area is built from bricks.

She pays 50 rupees a month to take water from the pipeline. Toilet visits are also expensive at 1 rupee per visit.

Between five and six every morning, Naseema gets up and makes breakfast tea for the family. She works from nine to twelve o'clock, then takes a break to make lunch. She used to work sorting strips of plastic but now she has been able to buy a sewing machine with borrowed money. She has managed to start a small business of her own and make a profit. She sews sacks for 5 rupees a piece. She tries to save 25 – 30 rupees a day, but if she cannot she will ask Preema to wait for a few days when she comes by on her daily visits. It is tough since she has installments and other loans to pay off. She paid 5,000 rupees for her sewing machine.

Her husband is an alcoholic. He used to have a juice stand but all of his assets are gone. Now he spends most of his time at his mother's house. He becomes violent when he drinks. Naseema's eardrum and back are permanently damaged because of his beatings.

SE

6:11 Naseema's blue house can be seen at the far end of the platform.

6:12 Naseema Banu with the family's goat. It is a family pet and supplies them with fresh milk.

RESHAM

6:13

In this image, Resham is standing in front of her oldest children. The two younger daughters are busy somewhere else. She is proud because she has just saved 40 rupees into her account with Mahila Milan.

The girl to the left does not belong to the family, her dress is very dirty and she does not look as confident as the other three. But we can see she understands the bank book that Resham is holding, is an important item. Perhaps the girl is deciding to get a book of her own.

Resham's clothes are clean and brightly coloured, and the same goes for her children. This implies that they have at least one other set of clothes, which signifies a certain material wealth. Resham works selling flowers with her family. Her husband is always in the city centre selling flowers and often when Preema comes to collect money for Mahila Milan, no one from the family is at home, they are all out selling flowers.

We can also see from the photograph that Resham is relatively young and that her children are teenagers. Resham must have been very young when she was married off and conceived her first child.

In the background we can also see how they live, it looks like a sort of temporary tent camp. They do not own much more than what they are carrying along with cooking utensils and a mattress to sleep on. Their home measures approximately 2 × 2.5 metres.

We can also see how close the trains are to where they live. They live right next to Mahim Station, precisely where the bombs exploded on the 14th of March 2006.

The nearest tap is on the other side of the station and they have to cross six busy railroad tracks every time they need to fetch water. Food is prepared over an open fire made from sticks and bits of collected scrap wood. There is no toilet.

SE

UJJWAL AND KAJAL DAS

6:14

During one of my long walks with Preema, I met Kajal and Ujjwal Das. Kajal had a big smile as she told me that she tried to save a couple of rupees every day.

Ujjwal is a fishmonger. He gets his fish from the market at dawn, then spends the day on foot, selling to his customers around the district.

When I visited them a year later their situation had become much worse. Ujjwal had broken his foot and could not work. Without social security or insurance, an accident or illness simply means that income ceases.

"We cannot save anything, our account is emptied and now we depend on neighbours and friends. Ujjwal does not have any money for medicine and his foot hurts." says Kajal.

Despite their predicament and Ujjiwal's constant pain, they invite me to take the step down into their home where they show me his x-rays. It is an ugly fracture.

The next day I am sitting on the bed sharing lunch with them. Delicious Chicken Masala – Kajal probably spent all morning preparing this unforgettable lunch.

SE

VIDA

We are sitting on simple, white plastic chairs in the pale glow of strip lights. We are in a common room in one of the transfer buildings for people who used to live next the railroad tracks of Mahim Station. A humming fan wisps back and forth and a small poster by the door tells us that we are welcome. The room works as a kind of office for SPARC.

The houses were built after negotiations between SPARC and the local railway company. SPARC showed them what the economical profit would be if they removed the shacks closest to the tracks. The Mumbai Railway Vikas Corporation made a deal where they would finance the re-housing of these people if, in return SPARC could guarantee that new homeless people would not try and establish themselves by the tracks.

At the age of seven, Vida moved next to the tracks by Mahim Station with her parents and her older brother. Their ten older siblings had died from various diseases. They had previously lived by the railway near Kings Circle. Their new home was approximately one metre from the tracks and as a child Vida was always frightened when the house shook from passing trains.

Life was dangerous. Just to fetch water or go to the toilet, they had to cross six tracks. During the rainy season, the shack would fill up with knee-high dirty water. The smaller children risked contracting diseases or even drowning when they played.

A few weeks after they moved to Mahim Station her father died, leaving her mother as the sole supporter of Vida and her brother. After school, Vida would work together with her mother, cleaning middle class homes. She attended school until the age of thirteen and then started working full time with heavy household work. At eighteen she married a man from the other side of the tracks. She tells us with a smile, that it was a love marriage and not an arranged one. She dreamt of leaving the slum and before her children were born she lived in Kuwait for two years, doing household work, but she was treated badly by her employer and decided to move back to a shack by the railway tracks, where she gave birth to her first child.

Before they could move into the new building, the people from Mahim Station had to stay in a transit camp. These eight-storey buildings were completed in 2000. A dark corridor runs through each floor. Some twenty doors on either side lead to each of the family's apartments. The apartments are approximately 25 square metres. Five to ten people normally live in these apartments, which consist of one large room, a partition and a kitchen. A few of the apartments also have their own toilets and showers.

When we visit Vida's building in the heat of the day, many of the doors are standing open, the drapes that hang inside each door post are swaying in the breeze. Around the doors, Hindu, Christian and Muslim symbols have been painted, showing individual family's religious beliefs. Inside some of the homes, women are sitting on the floor and working. Some are cutting loose thread from jeans or sewing and embroidering sari cloth and other material. In one apartment, a new born girl is proudly presented to us. The child's thick eye-liner will protect her against infections and the evil eye. The round black markings on her cheeks and in between her dark eyebrows also protect her against this curse.

Vida continues to tell us about her duties in the neighbourhood. At first we do not quite understand. She is not a police officer, but works for them. The police do not generally enter Dharavi at all. They prefer to let the Dharavians solve internal conflicts themselves as far as possible. After an agreement between the police, SPARC and Mahila Milan, local stations and offices have opened. They are run by reliable individuals in the local neighbourhood. Vida is one of them. She is employed by both the police and by SPARC, to keep order in the buildings that house former rail road dwellers. It's a sort of social service, rather than regular police officer work. In fact, she is respected and trusted, precisely because she is not a police officer people feel that they can talk to her about their problems and conflicts. Only in the most serious or violent cases are the police contacted. At the moment she is fully occupied by trying to trace a young couple from the building who have eloped. The girl's

6:15

family are threatening to call the police. Most of her work is trying to solve family conflicts. "First the children start fighting, then the mothers and then the fathers. By then a great fight between the families has broken out. Or a fight between parents-in-law. When we live on top of each other like this, friction is unavoidable."

Based on the violent riots in 1992, we ask, just as we have asked many others before, if there are any conflicts between the various religious beliefs. The answer is, as always – no.

"There is no prejudice of that kind here. We share the everyday and invite each other to our religious celebrations."

"This area is all joined" Vida exclaims when we suggest that we have heard condescending words about Muslims from Hindus. We find that our predefined categories based on religion, caste and region in India, from which the families originally have come, are too clumsy and general to give us any deeper understanding of what conventions regulate and govern the social life of Dharavi.

Before we say good-bye to Vida, we ask her about her thoughts on the relationship between men and women. Loud laughter fills the room when she asks why men do not have to ask for permission every time they leave home, or why they do not have to say where they have been or justify what they have been doing all day when they come home again. However strong women are, they always have to ask their men for permission before they can do anything, she says.

JW

Black Flags

On the 18th of June 2007 over seven thousand men, women and children gathered outside the offices of the Slum Rehabilitation Authority waving black flags in protest against the government's Dharavi Redevelopment Project. The black flags were not a statement of anarchy; they were meant as the opposite of a white truce flag. And their message was clear: "We will not surrender!"

The protest was a direct reaction to the advertisements that sought out global expressions of interest from real estate developers. The message of the black flags was that the people of Dharavi, the ones who actually turned this marsh into land, should be given priority in the redevelopment.

The protesting residents of Dharavi had three major demands:

Firstly, that the consent of 70 percent of affected slum dwellers should be made a mandatory requirement as in all individual slum rehabilitation projects.

Secondly, they demanded that the free tenements, which were being offered as part of the re-housing package, should be 37 square metres instead of the proposed 20 square metres.

And finally, the residents demanded that those who wished to undertake "self-development" like the potters of Kumbharwada, who have lived in the area since the 1950s, be permitted to do so.

The demonstration was peaceful and well organized. The protesters asked that their demands be passed on to the chief minister and that the clause requiring consent of the slum dwellers should be reintroduced in the project before entering a dialogue.

As Dharavi in many ways can be described as a township rather than a "pocket of slum", it should be treated as such. Dharavi stretches far beyond a limited geographical area. It has links to trade and commerce in the city of Mumbai and companies all around the world. There are more questions than those of housing and land at stake here. According to the organization Slum Dwellers International more than forty percent of the Dharavi inhabitants also work there. Dharavi is also a big employer for people from other parts of the city and the country.

The inhabitants of Dharavi do not want to stop development; on the contrary they are generally in favour of a better infrastructure. However, the black flags question the right of big business to violate ordinary people's livelihood and the assumption that they will be happy living in the 20 square metres they have been offered possibly far away from work. The promise of new apartments in high-rises are offered only to those who have formal papers on their properties, around 300,000. But for those without ownership, there are no offers at all. Moreover, the workshops and small businesses or the factories such as the printing industry are not taken into consideration. The people of Dharavi are deeply concerned about what will happen to their businesses during the development. Knowledge, experience and business opportunities might easily disappear in this transformational process.

Dharavi is not a green-field site waiting to be developed; it is the home and the workplace of hundreds of thousands of people. The black flag protest during the summer of 2007 demonstrates the organizational capacity of some of Mumbai's informal citizens. The inhabitants of this area have through this remarkably peaceful and well-organized manifestation proved that they want to remain an integral part of the city of Mumbai. If Dharavi is to be redeveloped this must be done in a way that works first for them, and then for the city, before others finally can start to make profit from it. Not the other way around.   *JHE*

Conventional planning approaches to slums and slum dwellers are thoroughly paternalistic. The trouble with paternalists is that they want to make impossibly profound changes and they choose impossibly superficial means for doing so. To overcome slums, we must regard slum dwellers as people capable of understanding and acting upon their own self-interests, which they certainly are.

JANE JACOBS

"The Death and Life of Great American Cities" (1961)

Dharavi is in the Midst of a Storm

by Sheela Patel

Dharavi is in the midst of a storm, as different development plans are proposed. Global capital investment companies, local real estate developers and the state government all envision Dharavi as the gateway to Mumbai's transformation. These proposals have crystallized opinion with all those associated to Dharavi. Mumbai is often called Slumbai or Slumbay; it probably has the largest number of slum-dwellers of any city in the world (over six million within the metropolitan area and many more outside). The current attention to Dharavi is the outcome of the Dharavi Redevelopment Plan which was drafted by the State Government of Maharashtra. Details of this plan and the objections raised to them are discussed at the end of this article. This is not the State's first attempt to redevelop Dharavi, but it is the latest one and if left unchallenged, it could threaten the lives and businesses of many residents.

THE BRIDGE THAT SPANS THE GAP

Some years ago, I was asked to explain my role in the alliance between SPARC, Mahila Milan (women's savings groups formed by slum and pavement dwellers) and the National Slum Dwellers Federation (NSDF). Of course one can give many answers, but in reality my overarching role and that of SPARC's remains twofold: first to assist grass roots organizations; second, to help slum dwellers secure their housing and other rights to the city. That role is like a bridge that spans the gap, because all negotiations between slum dwellers and external groups (including government agencies and private sector interests) keep going back and forth. Rarely are there any clear outcomes at the time. One must often look back to locate critical milestones when choices made led to vital outcomes, or events which occurred that washed away any gains made. In the case of Dharavi, SPARC is part of the group of Concerned Citizens for Dharavi (CCD) which is made up of professionals and activists and retired civil servants. This Group seeks to inform the State Government that neither residents of Dharavi nor residents of the Mumbai as a whole will not benefit from the present plans for Dharavi's future. NSDF and Mahila Milan are supporting their federation within Dharavi – The Dharavi Vikas Samittee (DVS) (Dharavi Development Committee) to align with other communities and networks who are equally unhappy with the present redevelopment plan. Over time a coalition has emerged which is known as Dharavi

Bachao Andolan (Movement to Save Dharavi) and these two organizations now represent the face of the resistance to the plan. So with communities in resistance mode, but still wanting development which works for them, our role remains to bridge the communication channels, to keep residents open to dialogue. What the results will be can only be described in the next edition of this book.

POOR COMMUNITIES AND INCREMENTAL HOUSING STRATEGIES

Poor communities generally want development, but are never included in that process as participants. They are always treated just as beneficiaries or consumers. In Dharavi the "beneficiaries" of the official development plan will not be the ones to reap the benefits of such investments. The slum dwellers inability to visualize planned change comes from years of opportunistic investment, below the official radar, made in their home and neighbourhood. Inch by inch they develop their spaces for homes and businesses and its conglomeration gives a character that we as outsiders see as Dharavi. This is a very vibrant conglomeration with tens of thousands of enterprises and hundreds of thousands of residents. Now suddenly, images of how this whole town within the city will be developed are presented by outsiders. These plans have been developed without any of the residents' involvement. Dharavi residents and businesses cannot locate themselves, their work and communities within such a visualization. It's as though, what they are familiar with, a gradual incremental evolutionary process, now fights with the new models of planning and development which devalues everything they do and have invested in. This is justified by claiming that Dharavi, as it stands, contravenes planning norms and building codes. In reality the drive to redevelop Dharavi is propelled by the very large profits that developers and the State Government will make.

Dharavi was built on marshes. First the houses had stilts, then land was reclaimed little by little, brick by brick. To those with a discerning eye, Dharavi is a testament to the innovative and survival instincts of the poor. Some even suggest that Dharavi should be given UNESCO heritage status because it stands as a historical monument of investment and design from below. Dharavi describes perfectly how most cities develop: the poor build their own homes, investing bit by bit, carving communities and neighbourhoods and finally towns as generations of families continue their work. When such flexible processes become incorporated in the norms of town planning, formalization occurs and over time, further upgrading produces legal and liveable spaces. Official support for these incremental processes are also signalled when the city provides urban infrastructure and services: clean piped water, sewage systems, good roads and social services, for example.

Poor people in urban settlements have often been neglected in the global South, and there is an increasing gap between the planned, formal city and its informal shadow. The gap in investments and the difference in house prices has become so wide in Dharavi that the city fathers cannot see how this might be bridged. Clearly financing systems which support incremental housing (most formal housing finance does not) must be used. There just isn't enough money available to replace these self built houses. De Soto states that a conservative estimate of all the informal housing in the world would far exceed the worth of the world's stock exchanges. This gap exists because there are no formal connections between the self built householder's capacity, aspirations and time frame to the official city. Ironically, official cities draw heavily on the labour and innovation of shanty town residents, but very rarely do cities support these workers. Without infrastructure provision or legal status, these communities will remain to be unable to move towards the formal, legal world via incremental development.

All of us who champion incremental development accept with some resignation that such possibilities in Mumbai are over. But not before we acknowledge three aspects that people have developed themselves.

First, that the residents have made huge investments in their own township development. This must be accepted by the state and by the financial and real estate interventionists, who at the moment are only offering compensation based on resettlement, not on the resident's lost investments.

Secondly there is a need to see Dharavi as a town within a metropolis, and not simply as a large slum. Walking through Dharavi, one sees a town in its own right, with social and cultural under-pinning, with multifaceted groupings of religions, residents from different states of India, and people with diverse beliefs and traditions. Dharavi is a vibrant town, with a complex physical, economic, social and cultural life, with multifaceted groupings of religions, castes, languages, provinces, and ethnicities, and a huge resources of social capital. Current redevelopment proposals treat Dharavi almost like a void or green field on which fresh lines and structures can be built, negating the deeply rooted habitat that already exists.

Thirdly, Dharavi is a vivid demonstration of entrepreneurial innovation in the face of global financial transformations. It has much to teach us about how informal settlements generate solutions to the demands of business and housing. Flexible work schedules, home-based occupations, businesses of various scales that interconnect with residences – this is the reality of how the poor not only survive, but thrive without handouts or charity. Regardless of development policies designed to keep the rural poor away from cities, people still flock to cities, even in the face of the dangers and trouble which might await them.

HOW THE PRIVATE SECTOR AND THE STATE VIEW DHARAVI

Some time in 2007 the Economist compared Kibera in Nairobi, Kenya (One of Africa's largest slums) and Dharavi. It was a comparison that got me thinking: what did the two townships have in common, apart from being large aggregations of informal dwellings with work spaces and homes? And it dawned on me that they represent two different dimensions of the relationship of poor communities to the state and the market. To the state they represent a long-standing development nightmare, for whom the state has not been able to develop any policies with which to upgrade and improve these large townships. Kibera and Dharavi are so embedded within their respective cities, that they serve as a constant reminder of the state's inability to create an inclusive model of urban development. But on the other hand, to the global financial institutions, they represent huge areas of well-located real estate. So as the Public Private Partnership (PPP) repeat to us again and again, the option of redeveloping these "eyesores" is too much to resist. The state will champion and enable their redevelopment by partnering market forces together, that will unleash the "true market value" of these sites.

Global financial investors still don't have the knowledge or capacity to manage decentralized, staggered investments which communities in Dharavi have evolved into a fine art. And new policy is not forthcoming from city planners to legitimize this approach and reduce the risks of lending to the poor. Global funding and real estate development have produced a one dimensional formula in which business houses borrow and repay capital. Hopefully, some time in the future, research, practice and activism will produce an alternative model which can be used to create financial mechanisms that support incremental development.

Gentrification is inevitable in large cities, but it is the real estate market and poor people in search of affordable space who shape cities far more than the planners. The poor inhabit the shadows and margins, creating value where none existed. They come into the public eye when the city expands around their settlements, which is when formal real estate begins to look at the land they occupy. Values of properties in a particular location transform neighbourhoods and push existing groups of households and communities to other places. Dharavi's neighbouring district of Bandra Kurla , the new business district with very high value commercial real estate, for instance, has pushed the Dharavi development into a frenzy of speculation. Dharavi was once a fishing village on the backwaters of one of the seven islands, on the periphery of Mumbai. Now, if cleared, it would be among the most valuable real estate in the world.

So one also needs to examine the pace of gentrification. Are there better ways to manage this? How gradual should it be? Who should benefit, and can this be part of the regulatory framework to ensure the vulnerable are protected from predatory speculation? How will such frameworks be developed? Who will enforce them? Can Mumbai lead the way?

DHARAVI'S STATUS TODAY (MARCH 2008)

Writing any reflections on Dharavi's redevelopment is difficult because the situation here is constantly changing. This book will freeze Dharavi in a single point in time. While this may be useful from a historical perspective, as it captures a range of perspectives around a given event, it is severely limiting for someone who is engaged in a struggle with the future.

There are many possible outcomes for Dharavi. The Government of Maharashtra was originally in a state of denial about the discontent of the residents, but now it accepts the need to heal that breach and listen to the residents' recommendations. Clearly that is not enough. Those who criticise the current strategy are being challenged to come up with better plans. But both residents and professionals acknowledge that unless new ideas emerge from a collaborative process, they will only mimic the old mistakes. Dharavi residents and dissidents don't want to stop the development or investment, they simply want to ensure that it will work for them as much as for the city at large.

Examining the power of citizens' associations, is always essential when such projects come under public scrutiny. Some claim that until the "trouble makers" (read that as activists from outside Dharavi) entered, all was well. There are even suggestions that civil society organizations and grass roots organizations only support such dissent to make money and further their reputation. I get asked this question by every TV crew that comes to shoot Dharavi for their documentary and news program. My answer is always the same, what fame and what money? My reflections on this take me to review the power of association. The complete non-acceptance of dissent from within the very people whose homes and lives are being affected by this development goes to the heart of the crisis of modern development practices. The views of the poor are not heard, recorded or acknowledged unless they are accompanied by voices from the mainstream or through violence. Violent dissent has become one of the only ways to reject state plans or market forces. It is an unfortunate side effect of a government which increasingly relies on inequity and exclusion to govern its people.

We are discovering increasing problems as the struggle for equality continues. Voluntary organizations are often accused of trouble making, when in reality they are simply delivering messages of dissent from those without a voice in the political arena. Some organizations are extremely suspicious of government practices feel that almost any dialogue with the state is problematic. In a process like Dharavi's development, where the outcome will affect hundreds of thousands of people, the stakes are very high. If there are mistakes in the redevelopment, the damages will be huge and irreversible. What is needed is cautious reflection and consensus building, but few politicians are willing to let themselves be this vulnerable.

When I speak at workshops and conferences there are many discussions about "world class cities". If we get the solution right to Mumbai's development, this city could be world class, it could lead the world on the issues of addressing inequality in housing. Mumbai may be the financial capital of India, but it has very little else to claim except in negative terms. But with every crisis comes an opportunity, it may have the largest number of slums in the world, but it also has a huge force of mobilized citizens, who are socially active across classes and localities. Mumbai has the potential to develop a world class model for slum redevelopment through consensual, increment building. All the ingredients are there. The true challenge is only whether the political leadership has the courage to explore it. We believe it is possible.

It's very gratifying to hear that so many people around the world care about Dharavi. Our situation seems to have really stirred the imagination of a wide range of academic institutions, documentary makers, researchers, journalists and young people. Sympathetic accounts of Dharavi's bustling commercial success and entrepreneurial innovation have even appeared in The Economist, Time and National Geographic. Getting international support for such a local crisis has really helped us contest the development process, especially now that so many international investors have become involved. Dharavi is sending out a strong message to the world, day after day demonstrating its imaginative responses to the problems of survival. Dharavi is being used by many as a template for the situations which many cities will faces in the coming years of rapid urbanization.

The local leadership in Dharavi receives a visiting delegation almost every day. But such engagements also have their downsides. Dharavi residents don't like developmental tourists, and with good reason too. On one occasion when there was a large conference in the city and organizers encouraged participants to visit Dharavi, those who did, later talked about it as though they had visited a dangerous war zone. But this reaction was countered by others who had come to listen, not just to stare. These people wanted to help, they wanted to write in international publications, make exhibitions celebrating Dharavi, they wanted to take home their impressions of a powerful self determination that has produced vibrant neighbourhoods and an amazing township. These visitors don't want to see such spirits dampened or destroyed by government ignorance.

Our association with students and staff from the Royal University College of Fine Arts in Stockholm began when they first visited us two years ago in 2006. And like other groups who were deeply moved by what they saw, they came back to explore the politics of inclusion and exclusion. They used their experiences to teach, to examine a different cultural environment from their own and to help students relate to their own past. 100 years ago, Sweden also had extensive slums and went through a rapid redevelopment. What is special about this relationship is that it is with artists who generally do not inhabit this particular field. They have decided to create this book and many other artistic productions. This is new for us and for residents of Dharavi. I look forward to finding out more about how globally connected relationships can help encourage inclusive development which is both locally driven and locally accountable.

MARCH 2008

The May 2007 letter from the Concerned Citizens for Dharavi was addressed to the Chief Minister of the State Government of Maharashtra, since the Dharavi Redevelopment Project is organized and managed by the state government. The following is an extract from this letter, followed by a summary of the issues it raised:

I am writing to you on behalf of several organizations – including academic institutions and NGOs – as well as on behalf of different individuals who are concerned with the Dharavi Redevelopment Project (DRP) as it stands today … In this letter we will list the issues which concern us, raise certain objections to the present DRP, ask certain questions and make certain recommendations as to a future roadmap. We are aware that the Government of Maharashtra has sanctioned the DRP but we feel that it should be scrutinized afresh. The people of Dharavi are largely ignorant about DRP, but those who are aware of it oppose it very fiercely. As a group, we are concerned that if the legitimate aspirations of the people of Dharavi are not met, their anger will spill out onto the streets … In order to avoid such a possible confrontation, it would be prudent to have a thorough re-look at DRP. Our issues are listed below.

A. LEGAL ISSUES

The DRP does not conform to the legal requirement for a Special Planning Authority to prepare and publish the draft plan and proposals for inviting suggestions and objections. This Plan is in effect an attempt to implement an existing Development Plan, but with a change in the Floor Space Index (FSI).

It would be incorrect to go ahead with the existing Development Plan which is completely out of date. There have been so many changes within Dharavi in terms of the number of people living there, the number of structures there, the kinds of activities undertaken today, the programmes implemented such as the Prime Minister's Grant Project and the increased connectivity of Dharavi with the rest of the city.

B. SURVEY AND DATA COLLECTION

One of the key issues for Dharavi's redevelopment is the extent to which it serves those who live and work in Dharavi – for instance, exactly who is entitled to be rehoused (and in what form and where) and what provisions are made for their enterprises or workspace? The exact population of Dharavi is unknown and the census data for Dharavi and the figures used by the Slum Rehabilitation Authority (that is in charge of the redevelopment) do not match. The basis for the Authority's estimation of 57,000 tenements in Dharavi is also not known. The basis for setting who is eligible for "resettlement" is also unclear – for instance a person or family's eligibility for rehousing might require that they have proof that they were residents at the beginning of 1995 or the beginning of 2000. Obviously, which date is chosen and what kind of documentation is required for proof have major implications for the number of "eligible" families. Our own population projections based on Census reports suggest that the numbers are much larger than estimated by the Dharavi Redevelopment Project. If the population of Dharavi is unclear, it will be difficult to plan for its redevelopment. Only a Baseline Demographic-cum-Socio-Economic Survey, which is open to public scrutiny, can give us the absolutely essential data needed for planning.

The number of structures in Dharavi has not been determined. The various purposes that each of these structures are used for (such as Residential, Residential + Commercial, Industrial, Religious, Educational and Health) are not known. If any survey has been conducted, its methodology has not been published, nor have its findings. There is a need for an infrastructure survey to assess existing conditions and the extent and nature of deficiencies.

The Dharavi Redevelopment Project does not present any data on ownership which can help to establish the pockets that can be redeveloped and those that have to be left out.

No detailed physical survey showing the topography of the Dharavi area has been carried out. This has particular importance because large sections of Dharavi are prone to flooding. Thus this survey is much needed to establish natural drainage systems, flood prone areas and soil conditions, which are critical in any planning for redevelopment.

C. PROJECTION STUDIES AND PLANNING STANDARDS

The increase in Dharavi's population that will be brought about by the "sale component" (as developers are granted permission to increase floor space ratios within Dharavi which means more commercial and residential space will be for sale). The implications on required land use distribution, amenities, infrastructure, traffic and urban forms have neither been understood nor carefully assessed. It is only on the basis of these projections that strategies for the design of the master plan can be conceived. For example, without projections for the increased volume of vehicular traffic, people and commercial activities, there is no basis for traffic planning.

D. PLANNING, DESIGN AND DISSEMINATION

An existing Land Use Survey needs to be undertaken and a proposed Land Use Plan prepared and published. Objections and suggestions for modifications to this have to be invited. Not only is this mandatory under law, it also becomes a way of involving the community and its representative organizations in the planning of Dharavi. This Land Use Plan also needs to show how Dharavi residents are going to be accommodated on 65% of the land. At present, Dharavi residents are not aware about where they will be resettled: for example, this might be in the worst low lying and flood prone areas of Dharavi. The proposed Development Plan shows that some sectors have less area assigned to rehousing the residents than others and this does not seem to reflect the population densities in these sectors. There is a concern that some sectors will have higher densities and taller buildings for rehousing than others.

There are concerns about what increase in Floor-Space Ratio should be permitted. This is one of the core concerns for the Redevelopment Project because the higher the Floor Space Ratio permitted (or what is sometimes termed the "bonus FSI" permitted to the developer), the more apartments or commercial buildings the developers can build for sale. But the higher the FSI permitted, the greater the likelihood that the residents will be rehoused in high-rise blocks and the less the provision per person will be for public amenities including open spaces, footpaths and educational and health facilities. We recommend that the government look at methods by which densities can be reduced, which means a reduction in the bonus FSI offered to the developers of each sector. One of the great attractions of the DRP for government agencies was that it needed no government funding (the developers would cover all the investment costs because of the profits they could make on these developments); indeed, the DRP as conceived at this time promised very substantial funding coming from the redevelopment for the government.

It would be possible for the government to break even with only a 0.25 bonus FSI, much lower than what is currently proposed. The government has to make a careful choice between the densities and the profits, in order to achieve a humane living environment.

The present DRP does not deal in depth with strategies for land use, traffic, urban form, infrastructure, housing typologies, and environment. One example of this is the hint that Dharavi may be served by a new metro system but there is no detail about its likely route and the corresponding locations of stations. Obviously, these routes and locations would be a key influence on Dharavi's land use pattern.

The Dharavi redevelopment model divides Dharavi into a few sectors, completely ignoring the existing "community" boundaries based on nagars. These have evolved over the years from community claims over property, occupations such as tanneries and religious boundaries. Existing nagar boundaries must be central to the planning process.

There is no coherent plan to link up the proposed infrastructure in Dharavi with the city's infrastructure. If individual developers take on the development of the sectors they are assigned, how can it be ensured that they fit in with the infrastructure provided by the Municipal Corporation? For example, if nallas (natural drains) are diverted or built upon, it could lead to a flooding emergency as has happened in Mumbai in the recent past. A plan for linking Dharavi's proposed infrastructure with that of the areas outside of Dharavi needs to be prepared, with a clear definition of roles and responsibilities between the Special Planning Authority, the different government agencies and private developers.

We note with surprise that this huge project involving more than 500,000 people and a planned investment of more than Rs. 9,000 crore [around USD 4.5 billion] has no Environmental Impact Assessment and suggest that this Assessment must be done at the township level and commissioned by the Government rather than by individual developers for their own "sectors".

E. ISSUES REGARDING LACK OF CLARITY OF PURPOSE OF THE DRP

Alternative development scenarios for Dharavi show that a much lower incentive FSI can still allow the development to break even financially but with much lower densities and with four storey [ground plus three] or five storey [ground plus four] buildings instead of high-rises. Our contention is that if the purpose of the project is to redevelop Dharavi without the Government of Maharashtra spending money, it is possible to do so by even offering 0.25 incentive FSI. We feel that enabling huge profits for the developers and huge revenues for Government of India should not be the main purpose of the project. As an extension to this argument, there is also no need to increase the cap of permissible FSI to 4.0.

Although the Government claims that the Dhararvi Redevelopment Project is a project initiated by the Government of Maharashtra, all tasks of conducting surveys, planning, design and construction have been left to private developers. The Government's role of negotiating and reconciling the interests of various groups, including its own interests, public interest and that of the community, has not been fulfilled. The role of Government as arbitrator needs to be spelt out.

One of the justifications for allocating Dharavi a higher FSI is that this is the only way of attracting developers to a "difficult area." But now that Dharavi is being redeveloped as a township and considering its extremely advantageous central location with excellent overall connectivity, the redevelopment of Dharavi would be very lucrative even with a much lower bonus FSI. Dharavi is also very close to the Bandra Kurla Complex, which commands some of the highest real estate prices in the world. Thus, detailed financial planning has to be undertaken to establish the need and extent of the bonus FSI required for Dharavi Redevelopment Project.

F. LACK OF CLARITY REGARDING INSTITUTIONAL ROLES

The DRP is considered a Government project with partnership from private developers. But critical state functions such as master-planning, environmental assessments and the seeking of mandatory clearances have been handed over to the developers. It is not at all clear how the Government of Maharashtra can hold developers to account for their commitments. For example, the DRP claims that the developers will maintain the buildings in which the population is rehoused and pay for elevator maintenance for a certain number of years. What mechanism is there to enforce such an obligation? Roles need reassessment and contractual provisions must be clarified.

Similarly, the Plan speaks of providing various amenities such as schools and health centres, but there is no mention of who will establish and run these or how these will be made affordable for low-income groups, except for vague statements about some individuals promising to do some things. Also, it is doubted whether such facilities would be open to existing communities, as has been seen with many private developments on public lands. Memoranda of Understanding and commitments from public and private authorities to establish and manage the proposed amenities are needed, with guaranteed access for low-income groups. The Government of Maharashra should prepare a document spelling out clearly the roles and responsibilities of different public and private actors in the planning and implementation in DRP.

G. ISSUES REGARDING ABSENCE OF COMMUNITY PARTICIPATION

We feel that the Redevelopment Plan has not provided any space for community participation. This is surprising, since one of the main principles of democracy and development planning is the involvement of the community in its own development. The 73rd and 74th Constitutional

Amendments reflect the commitment of the Indian State to democratic decentralization and community participation, which has, unfortunately, been completely ignored.

The people of Dharavi have virtually no information about DRP, except that it is a sector plan. They do not know who is eligible for rehabilitation, what their entitlements are, the locations of the transit tenements where they will be housed while redevelopment takes place, and where their permanent accommodations will be. They do not know what measures to take to protect their livelihoods and what types of housing will be provided. Furthermore, many residents have larger families, thereby making the 225 sq. ft. space [the size of the resettlement apartment they are promised] inadequate for their purposes. Has the government considered making additional area available to them, either as a profit-sharing mechanism with the developers or as additional purchasable property? Similarly, should not the residential development (as a "free sale" component) by private developers have a mandatory component of lower and middle income housing?

We strongly urge the Government of Maharashtra to re-introduce the clause of consent, so that the people can become involved in the redevelopment process. In slum redevelopment plans, there is a requirement that 70 percent of the population agree to the redevelopment, but the government has claimed that no such consent is needed in this case because the DRP is part of an already agreed development plan. The Government of Maharashtra should draw up a document to institutionalize community participation at every stage of DRP: surveying, planning, implementation, monitoring and evaluation.

H. OTHER ISSUES

There is a lack of clarity about exactly which land within Dharavi is to be within the Redevelopment Plan. There are some communities within Dharavi that appear to be within the plan in some documents or presentations and not in others. There are also some areas where a bonus FSI of 1,333 is not needed – for instance the communities staying in the municipal housing – since these are not high density and do not qualify as "difficult areas."

The letter ends:

In conclusion, we would like to say that the DRP needs to be examined afresh. In the light of the above objections/suggestions/recommendations, the Slum Rehabilitation Authority model itself may be unsuitable for Dharavi in view of its peculiar circumstances. An appropriate model needs to be developed. As a group, we would be happy to work with the Government of Maharashtra to prepare a road map for the development of Dharavi, that will be based on public scrutiny of all data; that will have the consent of the community; that will respect the links between housing and livelihoods; that will have diverse housing typologies to suit varied lifestyles and occupational factors as well as income groups; that will keep densities at manageable levels and restrict the role of developers to bidding for construction contracts. It should be possible to develop a low rise, high density settlement at Dharavi that keeps maintenance costs low and liveability conditions high.

SUNDAR BURRA

Explanatory text in square brackets has been added by the editors to help clarify certain points for readers unfamiliar with some of the issues raised.

Note about FSI; see Burra, Sundar (2005), "Towards a pro-poor slum upgrading framework in Mumbai, India", Environment and Urbanization, Vol. 17, No. 1, pages 67–88.

The need for the developers to pay for elevator maintenance may sound relatively trivial but it is a good example of the difficulties in supporting city redevelopment in ways that benefit low-income groups. Past experience with rehousing low-income households in high-rise buildings showed that actually, paying for the electricity to run the elevators and the service costs was a problem – to the point where in some high-rise developments, the elevators were not used. The problems this presents for families living on upper floors are obvious.

The Necklace of Dharavi

Soni Kadam, 17 and Saraha Kadam, 18 make an appointment with Anna and me. The sisters want to show us where one of their relatives runs a business. We take our cameras and they take us on a serpentine route through narrow alleys in parts of Dharavi we have never been to before. Pretty soon we start to feel very lost. Eventually we reach a small open space, a yard. The Kadam sisters point out a steep stairway among the surrounding stone houses. We climb up to the second floor together and find ourselves in a dark room. We are immediately struck by the heat from a couple of large stone ovens. A kind of snack that is offered in restaurants all over Mumbai is being fried in large iron-cast pans. In the corner, we see a boy crouching down next to a large pile of prepared snacks on the floor, pouring them into bags. The heat is almost unbearable and the air is heavy with dust. All the people working there are children.

When climb back down and stand in the yard, a young woman comes out from one of the houses and begins to scold Soni and Saraha for bringing us here. A quarrel breaks out that Anna and I cannot understand. We ask for an explanation and the young woman makes it clear that she is very upset that the girls have shown us this kind of activity. Her name is Suma, and she questions why they have to show us the worst side of Dharavi. She says that we are putting the young men's jobs at risk. The owner might become angry and sack people for this. Suma wants to know who has given Soni and Saraha permission to show us around.

Frightened and deeply shocked, the sisters take us out of there. They do not want to tell us any more about what the young woman said during the dispute. Never before had they been so humiliated or spoken to with such rude,

cursing language. We quickly return to a more familiar neighbourhood. Anna and I try to understand this hostility. Suma's violent accusations intrigue us, it makes us so curious that we decide to find our own way back.

A few days later we muddle along through the alleys without the Kadam sisters. Our return surprises Suma, and pretty soon a conversation starts up again.

Suma says, "The owner was asking about you and why you were filming. I just told him that you wanted to start your own dot-com and all, you were only taking observations to experience what we are doing."

"So, what happened?" we ask.

"Nothing happened." Suma says.

"So the owner …"

"Here is the owner." she says.

"Oh, hello. Maybe we should explain why we are here." I say.

Anna, Suma and I embark on a long discussion about the global economy, informal economy and micro-credits. Despite our different perspectives, we do agree upon the general analysis – which surprises us with our preconceived and slightly patronising ideas of how Suma, a young woman in the slum of Dharavi, with no formal schooling at all, can reason about the complicated relationships between the rich world and the poor. Suma stresses how we share these problems by pointing out that we all are consumers. The people in the slum do not only produce but also consume these cheap products. Thereby we all must share responsibility for sending young children to work. Throughout our conversation Suma's glass bangles clink together, and as she argues she refers to the terrible circumstances in which young girls

6:16 Suma with her mother and son.

make the very same kind of glass bangles she herself loves to wear. "We are the elders, we are making them work like that. But nobody knows the problems that we are facing" she says. "We share the responsibility of child labour. We also have a common responsibility to make sure that Dharavi is represented faithfully." She continues, "the other day I told you: 'Don't shoot me like an object.' If you want to shoot me, you should bear my problems, take my problems as if they were yours. To understand my problems you should film me, but don't shoot me like an object."

The questions that arise are all to do with how we, as Westerners, can find a way to tell the stories of Dharavi faithfully, without misrepresenting the people who live here. In the same gesture the people of Dharavi are supposed to admit the hardships and wrong doings in their own neighbourhood as well as stand up for the community, for Dharavi. An everyday struggle for one's self-esteem. How can one be proud about the quality of products produced in Dharavi without denying the child labour, low wages and unhealthy workshops which are polluting the city? Every morning, the women try to keep their communities clean, as no one else does, so that they can sit and work together and let the children play. Abandoned as they are by the municipality and the politicians, keeping the neighbourhood clean is an important aspect of self-representation and self-esteem. The border between the private house and the public space is not always easy to discern. Visitors must keep this in mind, and must expect questions when they intrude.

"We don't know who is coming. All we know is that there is child labour and that people are coming to look. Ok, we have child labour. If a child is working we should put the company owner in jail. I thought you were coming for child labour only. In every business they are forcing the children to work, that is the situation over here. Even the owner is a child, he is not eighteen. That is why I thought, 'Oh God, what is happening!' Because you see, three years ago the police, the constables came and took the children. We should not work like this. If you want to work in peace you should work with elders. Child labour is very illegal." Suma says.

"But now you are working in the police station, you told us and you knew about this, don't you feel that you should report it?" we ask.

"Yes, but I am in a very low position and I don't have the right to speak to my seniors. If I speak to seniors I don't know what kind of senior he is. Suddenly he might question me: 'Why are speaking of this? That is my duty, I will see to their problems. I am the senior, I will communicate with them.' I just don't have the right to speak to my seniors because I am in a lower post. I just have to respect my seniors, to salute my seniors."

Being a strong-willed young woman in Dharavi is full of contradictions. Suma continually points out that everything she has achieved has been a battle against forces that would rather have her passive and silent.

"Dharavi is my family. We are the necklace of Dharavi. We are the crown of Dharavi. I don't want to show myself as a useless person. My Dharavi is best. I give you fine goods, fine clothes. Even in simple houses the women are working. For what? – because nobody is helping them, they are doing it for their own family."

No matter how much Suma is raising her voice for Dharavi, no matter how much the women in the neighbourhood are cleaning up, someone and something always shows up to undo whatever they are striving for.

"They are greedy persons. The company owners have the money and do not care about the problems that we are facing. They put up the factories and workshops and you can see how much garbage they are throwing out. They contaminate our water and you can smell it. We cannot speak to those people as they have the rights and the law. We have no rights and no law, and we don't have the support that they have. Now you are recording my voice, and if they will hear about it they will ask me why I spoke up like that."

When we ask why she does not go into the politics she sighs deeply before explaining that the politicians would never let her in since she would speak against them as she represents the lower castes and the women of Dharavi, and that the political chairs are too precious for those who are already occupying them.

Throughout her life Suma has been met with disrespect, both because she is a woman and also because of her low caste. She has always been placed in the lowest positions. After many hardships, Suma finally got a professional education. Her mother was very supportive. Suma was full of pride when she got the job with the police, but once again found herself at the bottom of the chain of command. Working as a police officer she became a home guard without any position or possibility to have her voice heard.

"If a woman is working as a constable, people will not show her any respect. They will just tell you to go and sit over there, even in rude language."

Now a married woman with children of her own, Suma refuses to be silenced and subdued by her roles as a mother and wife. Suma's mother has always stood up for her, even against the will of her father. "That which I could not do, my daughter is doing now" her mother used to say. Affectionately, Suma expresses all the esteem and respect her mother deserves. Her mother never got any education and she did not want her daughter to go through the same kind of problems that she did with her own family. A legacy Suma will pass onto her own daughter, "a woman will only be helped by other women."

"If you are having a problem you should only share that with another woman, and not with a man. If I would tell my problems to a man he will only create more problems. He would insult me, tease me, but women are not like that. If you have a will you must follow that will and not just stay home to do the housework."

Suma vividly depicts the different roles women are forced into from early childhood onwards, the rules and customs which prevent women from following their own will and convictions. Referring to the sign "Beware of the dog", Suma laughingly urges young women to think "Beware of the family" unless they want to get caught and curtailed by their father, husband or mother-in-law.

"Even if people are telling you that you have no right to help other people, you have no right to stand up against the authorities and the police. If you care for democracy, if you have the power to do things for the people, for Dharavi, you just have to do what you must."

"But do you talk with you friends about this?" we ask.

"Oh yes many times, but they just say that they don't have the power as their families are not with them in the way that my family stands behind me."

We are sitting outside Suma's house in the little square that the women clean every morning. As we speak children are playing around our feet. Shyly, or reserved, the men are standing in the background listening. The women are sitting in a circle close by, working with whatever is at their hands. Street vendors are passing by, shouting out the goods they are offering.

"What do you think about your future? If you could just dream of anything what would it be?" we ask.

"I want to become prime minister."

"Good, then be one!"

"If I become prime minister the women will be on top of the world. And I will not sit on the side, I will struggle and struggle for my country."

JW

LEARNING BY DOING

This book has been an entirely collaborative project. We are a group of head-strong individuals who have managed to use each other's expertise when grappling with the many new questions which we encountered. Mutual trust and sharing have been the main tools which we used when working with our friends in Mumbai and Dharavi.

However, in many respects we are amateurs in regard to the questions that are poised in this book. But we are also amateurs in the sense of being passionate, curious, and unafraid to ask naïve questions. We did not visit Dharavi to teach, but rather to learn. This perspective has been of the utmost importance.

The group, in alphabetical order:

SOPHIE ALLGÅRDH *(SA)*

As editor-in-chief of the Swedish art publication Paletten and critic at Svenska Dagbladet (one of Sweden's national newspapers), I am interested in the complex relationship between contemporary art and politics. I recently curated the 2007 Öyvind Fahlström retrospective at Mjellby Konstmuseum. This reflected my enthusiasm for socially conscious art.

The trip to Dharavi has enabled me to learn more about the context surrounding contemporary Indian Art.

STINA EKMAN *(SE)*

I have been working as an artist for over a quarter of a century. In the nineties I was appointed professor of fine arts, specialising in sculpture. I taught for ten years in the very north of Sweden as well as in Stockholm, spending short periods of time abroad. My works have been exhibited in 17 countries.

What kind of world was I born into?

What it is to be a human being?

In Dharavi I learned that "we" and "them" should be replaced. "Us together" is the way, no matter where on earth we stay.

JONATAN HABIB ENGQVIST *(JHE)*

I co-edited and translated this book, but my interest in this project has always been from the point of view of a philosopher and aesthetic theorist. For me this project has been very much about relationships. Relationships to the people in the group, to the people of Dharavi and to the various organizations we have received help and advice from. It has also evoked more general, philosophical questions concerning spatial experience. I think that on a fundamental level we all perceive space in a very relational way. This experience is intensified when physical space becomes a luxury item.

We have a lot to learn from the creative solutions in high density areas like Dharavi. Not only from a structural, relational or existential points of view, but also (considering the accelerating development of technology, globalization and recent environmental changes) we had better start listening carefully to those who know how to make their lives sustainable whilst manoeuvring through our own parallel landscapes of relationships.

LOVE ENQVIST *(LE)*

I am an artist based in Stockholm who has studied in Stockholm, Frankfurt and Helsinki. I'm fascinated by projects that try to turn dreams into reality. Utopian communities and theories have often informed my work about embodied, urban experience.

As an artist, I believe it was my responsibility to learn from Dharavi, to let the experience filter into my life, rather than to use Dharavi as just a way to express my own agenda. By studying Dharavi's architecture and by reflecting on how the inhabitants' lives and my life are related, I have brought back a wealth of ideas and questions which I hope to pursue.

More than anything, this project has meant that the word "we" has taken on a new significance for me. By using collective action and acknowledging one's own significance within society, the people of Dharavi are creating powerful grass roots organizations which we in Sweden would do well to replicate.

ANNA ERLANDSON *(AE)*

I am an artist, educated at Umeå University College of Fine Arts. The intense trip to India was the beginning of a new way of understanding the world. Changing the way one interprets the world implies a long and profound process of relearning. Deconstructing preconceptions and habitual logics is a slow and even frustrating process. It is in the meeting face to face, the mutual sharing of time and stories, where little by little, pieces fall together and a complex map of similarities and connections is revealed. Dharavi has taught me that change is possible, and the change cannot wait.

With this book as a ground, we proceed into the project Informal Cities, where voices from six countries contribute to our mutual and never-ending story about the city and the people living in it.

JAKE FORD *(JF)*

As well as working as a landscape architect in Stockholm, I also co-run Medium, a studio producing projects related to public space, architecture and visual culture. Medium projects often focus on the context of our everyday lives, the commonplace things that often go unnoticed. Medium works with an international network from visual arts, communication design, architecture and product design. During this project my perception of Dharavi has changed massively. The last visit to Dharavi has shown potential links between the huge recycling industry, micro-credit organizations and collective building projects.

JONAS JERNBERG *(JJ)*

I am an architect and urban planner. I am one of five co-founders of the architectural office N59 architects in Stockholm. My main interest is in informal urban structures and the different characteristics of self-made housing and unplanned space. In a broader perspective I am interested in political and social issues connected to the physical environment.

Among other things, my experience from this trip engaged me in the process of forming a Swedish Architecture Sans Frontières, ASF Sverige.

MARTIN KARLSSON *(MK)*

I am an artist and my work often implies different kinds of documentary practices like photography. I have a special interest in history. Whilst visiting Dharavi I became fascinated by the changes that are taking place and what the future holds for the area. The disparities between the government's blueprints for Dharavi and the inhabitant's everyday experience made studying the area of interest both on the individual level and also on a wider, political level. Certain families who have lived in very simple conditions, perhaps even on the street are now being offered the chance to move into high-rises with relatively high standards of living. Will this change the status of Dharavi? How will this effect people's daily lives and in the long run – their own sense of self? The demolition work and new building projects will totally transform Dharavi, and perhaps the divisions between the formal and informal will become even more blurred.

MARIA LANTZ *(ML)*

I am employed as a senior lecturer at the Royal University College of Fine Arts in Stockholm Sweden. In this institution, I am in charge of the multi-disciplinary research program Art & Architecture which was the point of departure for the first mutual journey to India. A journey which, among other fortunate circumstances, made this book possible.

I am also an essayist on photography for the morning paper Dagens Nyheter and the image editor of Motiv, a magazine on contemporary photography. However, these occupations are the result of my background as a photographer, an occupation I still love and work within. These days I work with my own collaboration projects which are always related to urbanism and the global, informal life which connect all of us.

MONIKA MARKLINGER *(MM)*

One of my strongest impressions from Dharavi was the orange Hindu and the green Muslim streamers which stuck up wherever I looked. As a painter I was struck by the muddle and the cultural diversity of Dharavi. Contemporariness is not just a keyword for the structure of collage making but signifies Dharavi as well. Electric cables connect the temples with the recycling-stations and spread like a mycelium over this site filled with ambiguity and contradictions.

In my pictures from Dharavi I try to intertwine my own individual language with the reproducible expressions of society. The claim for veracity implicitly included in photography is challenged and called in question by the inevitably subjective perspective of drawing. In that sense my aim is not only to expose my own position of dependence in a society which to an increasing extent reclines on the informal sector. By erasing the limit between the documentary and the fictive I try to create new outlooks on the informal settlements which host so much hopelessness but also so many dreams.

JOHAN WIDÉN *(JW)*

Professor of fine art, specializing in painting and Pro-Vice-Chancellor at the Royal University College of Fine Arts, Stockholm. Johan is involved in the multi-disciplinary department Art & Architecture.

The goal of this department is to create an international forum for contemporary discussions in art, architecture, technology, and community planning. The program is aimed at artists, architects, engineers, photographers and journalists.

ACKNOWLEDGEMENTS

Anders Wilhelmson, professor of Architecture in Stockholm who began everything with the obnoxious "take me to India"-request back in 2004, when the idea of learning from the slums took root at the Royal University College. *Andrew Preston,* UK, through whom we were introduced to the Society for the Promotion of Area Resource Centers (SPARC). *Sundar Burra,* SPARC, who took his time to show us their work and *Sheela Patel,* SPARC, who encouraged us to continue the collaboration between North and South and also contributed with a key piece in this book.

Professor *Henrietta Palmer* and the Dean of the Royal University College of Fine Arts, *Marie-Louise Ekman,* for suggesting one semester of project time.

Shenaz and *Hemlata* for translating for the team in Dharavi. *Jockin* for spending his precious time with us.

Preema for taking us on her walks for Mahila Milan, *Shirish B Patel* and *Katia Savshuck* for proof-reading. Thanks to *Thomas Melin* at SIDA for his engagement and creative support. *Johan Rutherhagen* for structuring the vast material and transforming it into readable graphic design and *Mark McLaren* for more proof-reading.

Finally, we would like to thank *Professor Saskia Sassen* and *Professor Arjun Appadurai* for their brilliant contributions to this book.

We are most grateful for the generous support by both SIDA and *The Embassy of Sweden* in New Delhi.

ON BEHALF OF THE AUTHORS AND ARTISTS
MARIA LANTZ AND JONATAN HABIB ENGQVIST, EDITORS

6:17

6:17   Maria Lantz co-
ordinating and taking
photographs.

6:18   Love Enqvist playing
with the children of
Poonawalla.

FURTHER READING

BOOKS

APPADURAI, ARJUN
Fear of Small Numbers: An Essay on the Geography of Anger, Duke University Press, 2006.

BAUMAN, ZYGMUNT
Liquid Fear, Polity press, 2006

DAVIS, MIKE
Planet of Slums, Verso, 2006

KALPANA, SHARMA
Rediscovering Dharavi: Stories From Asia's Largest Slum, Penguin India, 2000

MEHTA, SUKETU
Maximum City: Bombay Lost and Found, Penguin India, 2000

NEUWIRTH, ROBERT
Shadow Cities: A Billion Squatters, A New Urban World, Routledge, 2005

SASSEN, SASKIA
A sociology of globalization. Norton, 2006
Territory, authority, rights: from medieval to global assemblages, Princeton University Press, 2006
The Global City. Princeton University Press, 1999

WEB

INFORMAL CITIES
www.informalcities.org

SDI SLUM/SHACK Dwellers International
www.sdinet.org

DISCUSSION BOARDS:
www.dharavi.org
squattercity.blogspot.com

This book was made with the kind assistance of:
SPARC
www.sparcindia.org

6:18

IMAGE CREDITS

© **SOPHIE ALLGÅRDH** 5:52

© **STINA EKMAN**
2:20, 2:21, 3:32–3:34, 4:12, 4:13, 4:16, 4:17, 4:26, 4:28, 4:31, 4:37, 4:45–4:47, 4:49–4:54, 4:62, 6:5–6:11, 6:13, 6:14

© **LOVE ENQVIST**
1:6, 1:7, 4:4, 4:27, 4:41, 6:2

© **ANNA ERLANDSON**
1:8–1:10, 1:15, 2:24–2:28, 3:3–3:5, 3:35, 3:36, 4:3, 4:7, 4:8, 4:11, 4:18, 4:24, 4:25, 4:29, 4:30, 4:34–4:36, 4:39, 4:42, 4:55, 4:57, 4:60, 4:61, 5:41–5:49, 5:52, 6:3, 6:4, 6:12, 6:15–6:18

© **JAKE FORD**
2:15–2:19, 3:20 – 3:30, 4:19–4:21, 4:23, 4:24

© **MARTIN KARLSSON**
2:22, 4:15, 4:32, 4:43, 4:44, 4:48, 5:2–5:40

© **MARIA LANTZ**
0:3, 1:5, 2:2–2:12, 2:23, 3:2, 3:6, 3:14–3:19, 3:31, 4:5, 4:6, 4:14, 4:33, 6:19

© **MONIKA MARKLINGER**
Cover illustrations, 0:1, 1:1 , 2:1, 3:1, 4:1, 4:9, 4:10, 4:38, 4:58, 5:1, 6:1

© **JOHAN RUTHERHAGEN**
Hard cover illustration (foil), 0:4

© **JOHAN WIDÉN** 3:11–3:13, 4:2

© **HILARY KOOB-SASSEN**
1:2, Still "The Paraculture"
(T+2 Gallery, London, UK 2005)

© **MAGESH MURUGAN** 1:10

© **B MANOJ** 1:12

© **SOFISTIC** 1:13

© **MAGESH MURUGAN** 1:14

© **ATISH KADAM** 5:50–5:51

© **NASA** 1:3

© **DIGITAL GLOBE / GOOGLE EARTH**
1:4, 3:7–3:10

6:19